# THE FIRESIGN THEATRE
## *Presents*
# ANYTHYNGE YOU WANT TO
## SHAKESPEARE'S LOST COMEDIE

## *&*

# "THE LEGEND OF THE FIRESIGN THEATRE"

4 OR 5 CRAZEE BOOKS

# ANYTHYNGE YOU WANT TO®

*YE OILEY SCRIPTE*

410th Anniversary Edition

**THE LONG-LOST COMEDIE**

PUBLISHED ACCORDING TO THE TRUE ORIGINAL COPIES

OFTEN CURIOUSLY ATTRIBUTED TO

## WM. SHAKESPHERE

(No performances in UK without license of Stratford Trust Bank)

TOGETHER WITH A SCHOLARLY INTRODUCTION,

*Highly Polished Footnotes and Swollen Appendices*

**FULLY ILLUSTRATED!!**

*And At No Extra Cost!!*

## "THE LEGEND OF THE FIRESIGN THEATRE"

ADDITIONAL DIALOGUE

For the Derrick Escrow Raadio Pflegm Production by

**RICK SHAKESPEARE**

(Universal Representation by The Greatest Agency of All)

DRAMATURGUED BY

**THE GREAT SHENANNIGAN**

(c) 1895 by Shenannigan Heir Group Ptnrs Ltd.

Additionally, Exactly as Performed to Great Acclaim By

**THE LEGENDARY**

## FIRESIGN THEATRE

**"WAITING FOR THE MOUNT OF COUNTY CRISCO,**

With Someone Like Him" — A *Commedia* Burlesque of the

Bros. Shakespeare's Tragical "Philip, Prince of Norway."

Plus! The Adventures of Dr. Firesign's Theatre of the Plains,

performing in *"Orphan's Tears," "The Armenian's Paw"*

and *"Everything You Know is Wrong!"*

**Copyright (c) 1974, 1980, 2011**
BY PHILIP AUSTIN, PETER BERGMAN, DAVID OSSMAN AND PHILIP PROCTOR

ALL RIGHTS RESERVED.

No part of this book may be reproduced in any form or by any means, electronic, mechanical, digital, photocopying, or recording, except for in the inclusion of a review, without permission in writing from the publisher.

Published in the USA by:
**BEARMANOR MEDIA**
P.O. BOX 71426
ALBANY, GEORGIA 31708
www.BearManorMedia.com

Early versions of the "Critical Introduction" and
"The Legend of The Firesign Theatre"
were published in *The Firesign Theatre's Big Mystery Joke Book*
Straight Arrow Books, 1974.

"Anythynge You Want To" was commissioned by *earplay* in 1980
for the final season of regular radio theatre on NPR.
An edited version was released in 1982 on LP by Rhino Records
under the title "Shakespeare's Lost Comedie."
Later CD issues are "Newly Found and Enlarged to Almost as Much Againe as it Was,
According to the True and Perfect Coppie."

"Orphan's Tears" first appeared in Crawdaddy.
"Shakespeare at Sea" first appeared in Foolish Times.
"The Armenian's Paw" performed on KRLA, Dec. 17, 1967.
Other material is referenced in FT's "Everything You Know Is Wrong"
album and film (1974-1975) and "Not Insane" (1973).

Original LP Album Art by Bruce Litz.
Dr. Firesign's Theatre and Ash Grove performance photos by John Rose.
"Orphan's Tears" photos by Alan Daviau, art direction by Bill Jones.
Rick Shakespeares by Phil Fountain. Orson Welles by Josh Weiner for "A Safe Place."
FJQ and Fighting Clones by Barrie M. Schwortz.
Feelgood portrait by Marv Lyons. Shortears portrait by Jerry de Wilde.
Original Dr. Firesign poster art by Thad Warrick.
Digital thanks to Taylor Jessen, Firesign Theatre's Archivist.

If you are interested in staging a production of
"Anythynge You Want To," "The Count of Monte Cristo,"
or any variant of these scripts, please apply in writing to
**FIRESIGN THEATRE RIGHTS**, P. O. BOX 566, FREELAND WA 98249.

The Firesign Theatre's website is **firesigntheatre.com**

ISBN-10: 1-59393-664-8 (alk. paper)
ISBN-13: 973-1-59393-664-8 (alk. paper)

Printed in the United States of America.

Cover photograph and character portraits by Oona Austin.
Cover design by Phil Fountain, Oz Design Group.
Edited by David Ossman.
Designed by Valerie Thompson.

First Edition.

*With renewed appreciation for our*
**Original Cast:**

**Ben Wright** *as "Your Host"*

**Diz White** *as "Marie"*

**Susan Tanner** *as "Second Weird Cook"*

**John Meyer** *as "Lord Mulholland"*

**Irregular Humorists of the Radio Extras Guild**, *Hollywood Local 28,*

*and for*

**Ron Patterson**, *Master of the Revels.*

*Coat of Arms of the Congress of Grave Makers and Coarse Actors*
(founded 1302).
*Popularly known as* **Ye Smoked Hammes.**

# CONTENTS

**A CRITICAL INTRODUCTION** to "Anythynge You Want To" . . . **1**

**"ANYTHYNGE YOU WANT TO"** BY WM SHAKESPHERE . . . **9**
*As Performed Somewhat Completely and Mostly Unabridged
With Additional Dialogue for Raadio Phlegm by* **Rick Shakespeare**

## APPENDICES

**ONE:** "Waiting For The Mount of County Crisco," as frequently performed by The Firesign Theatre. . . . **101**

**TWO:** "The Cloister Scene" from Ziegfeld's "Shakespeare's Follies of 1928" and "Sweet Marie's Mad Scene" from "The Suffragette's Shakespeare." . . . **117**

**THREE:** Program notes and interval features for the Pflegmish National Public Radio Broadcast (Raadio Pflegm, 1980). . . . **122**

**FOUR:** A Dramaturgical Analysis of the "Interactive Anythynge." . . . **127**

**FIVE:** Recipes from Chef Crockette's "Edible Shakespeare." . . . **132**

**SIX:** "Shenannigan! Shakespeare's Lost Comedy Exposed!" The documentary film version. . . . **137**

**SEVEN:** Additional Dialogue by Rick Shakespeare. . . . **143**

**EIGHT:** Shakesphere At Sea — An Interview with Rick Shakespeare and Location Jottings from Derrick Escrow. . . . **152**

## THE LEGEND OF "THE FIRESIGN THEATRE" . . . **158**

**ONE:** "The Count of Monte Cristo," as once performed by Dr. Firesign's Antique Theatre of the Plains, plus "Orphan's Tears" — Act One of the famous Melodrama. . . . **180**

**TWO:** Everything You Know Is Wrong about "Anythynge You Want To!" Finally, Harry Cox's unexpurgated story! . . . **193**

**THREE:** "The Armenian's Paw" — a Tale of Dr. Firesign's Theatre. . . . **205**

*The young Sir Jack Feelgood as Hambone Shallow
in a 1965 Holy Day Inne production of
"Devyls Wyves and Saylors Wysdome"*

# "ANYTHYNGE YOU WANT TO"
## A CRITICAL INTRODUCTION

BY PHILO GEMSTONE, FHD AND PETER SAVATTE, OD,
SOLID STATE UNIVERSITY,
DARLENE YUC A'AMOTO, DDS, MZ, FRESNO UNIVERSITY OF THE AIR,
AND ANTON SHORTHAIRS, SOB, VIRTUAL PROFESSOR OF 'PATAPHYSICS,
MILLIGAN UNIVERSITY AT LEEDS.

" . . . two bruddrs Ed or Eddy named, armes linkt and toasted gyblerts intertwyned, then dyed a singular gibbous deaff while t'others, clown Bishop wise and Addled Count, fhey uldd com so foon, dat all wuld bee Amuzed. Fyre they wuz, cuz, belikely the foonest jibsters dat La Quene hiffelf doth kommend dem. Fyre Sygne if da Thrtre ta see here in Lerndon." [1]

High praise from the pen of a marooned Dutch seaman named Jan Groot,[2] writing to his sisters back home in Pflegm of the pleasures of seventeenth-century London. Groot had probably witnessed a performance of the revenge comedy, *Anythynge You Want To*, on the courtyard stage of the Holy Day Inn,[3] across the Thames River in

---

[1] From *Groot's Dyaries*, reprinted in Mathewschild, Irving, *Fire and Shake In Medieval English Drama*. Oxx. U. Press, 1927. See especially Chapter 7, "Groot In Lerndon."

[2] Groot was Captain of one of the ill-fated "Hellburners," purchased from the Dutch to fight the Spanish Armada. Groot evidently misread his instructions, heading the wrong way and striking the Tower as the ship's fuses fizzled and finally flamed out. As Captain, Groot left the ship in a skiff, but misread the current and found his way to Deptford where he went ashore and attempted to blend into the crowd, hoping not to be prosecuted for his mistakes. A week later, the Hellburner blew up, wiping out a portion of the docks. The event was deemed "onlye a Foolysh jest" bu William of Lime, who supposedly then stated ". . . but not a very good one." It took Groot some 18 years, disguised, to make his way back to his native village of Spyttle in the Pflegmland of the Nethers. Butt that is a much longer story.

[3] The Holy Day Inn was built in 1529 on the site of the annual Holy Day Revels which brought together "throngs of lechers, paupers, defrocked clerics, whores and idiot savants," according to Godspit Gallowschild, the Lord Mayor of London at the time. The revelers chose a favorite saint and impersonated them with "energie, frivolitie and lack of Common Proprietie," as described by Martin Habit of Ginslingshire's remaining monastery. The celebrations drew enormous crowds, including a variety of fringe performers, among them an unidentified flame-swallower upon whose shoulders we can place the blame for the demise of the wildly popular "indulgencies." He unfortunately mixed heavy drinking with his art and,

Holy Wood, then as now a bristling suburb. This popular play is one of four[4] now commonly attributed to the members of a theatrical company, unusual not only for the times but as well, for all time. Unlike the usual theatrical troupe of the day, which numbered as many as forty players, the Fyre Sygne Thrtre was unique in that it only was comprised of four or five "men" (their exact number has frequently been questioned by scholars, so little is known of them[5]).

According to fire insurance records, only four names are exactly known, (although these may have been five) as "thee onely partissypants in these Mad Exercises"[6]— Paules Peeterboorg, a Pflegmish playwright and bear-hater[7]; Proctor Christman, the young son of the Archbishop of Arch and a poet of the "Nife and Kut" school[8]; the satirist Sackville Boozeman[9]; and finally, the mysterious Philip Phillip, who had apparently been reversed at birth[10], and is credited by some[11] with inspiring

---

while performing on the central stage, upchucked gouts of grog and flame that consumed the structure and took a shocking number of expendable lives. AS

[4] Goncort, Prosper and Gedwillo, Thomas, "Four or Five, It Doest Not Not Mattere," in Glib's *Critical Essays*, S. S. U. Press, 1969. This article condenses somewhat the many long arguments that have characterized the search for a so-called "Fifth Play," which may or may not exist. There are several contenders for this missing fifth, most notably *Homlette* by the original Wm. Shakespheare, and *Plotinus the Mad* by Christopher Marley, and as well, Greene's "Po'Ossum Lodge." (Comedon and Greene's *Trajedy of young Candidus* and Poley's *In Yr Yeye*, are hardly mentioned.} Wm. Shakespheare, by the way, is often promoted as the mysterious "fifth writer" in the Fyre Sygne Thrtre, especially upon the discovery of a sodden MS of *Anythynge You Want To* in the possession of a *soi-disant* descendant in America. (See Note 32.)

[5] See, for example, Faust's "Die Zoftigfrauleinsmotif von zu Feuersteinteater," and Henrik Ibid's "Oswald, Oswald, Where Ya Gun Lie Downe?" in the Special Issue of *Lancers*, October 27, 1964.

[6] [*sic*] "Groot's Dyarys."

[7] A native Pflegmlander, Peeterboorg was celebrated in bear-hating circles as a "Veritable Wizzard of Mis-Information." A charcoal drawing in the collection of the Royal Society depicts a grimacing Peeterboorg in the role of the Bishop of Pflegm, in costume and makeup of obviously Turkish origins, fleeing a bear. Peeterboorg was an active "beer-batterer" and one of the owners of the ancient Bearwhize Brewery of London. It would seem no small coincidence that Jan Groot, a fellow countryman, saw and perhaps even knew Peterboorg during his long captivity in London.

[8] Of Russo-French extraction, Christman was the "brawling foole" who declaimed his verse in taverns, whether or not the "nother customers enjoyned it or no," Groot notes. According to Trollope, he spent his later days "a gentle fellow, yet devilish as St. Nick."

[9] Much older than his companions, Boozeman had been a tuppeny versifier and sometime writer of humorous broadsides before becoming the "Alte Cocke vom dens FT," as Groot so cryptically writes in his "Dyarys."

[10] Philip Phillip may actually have been two different persons. On the other hand, no less an authority than Sig Fraud has suggested he, or they, were actually Siamese twins, probably of opposite, or at least of different sexes. If the "Two Phils" theory is true, however, as Prof. Pinedecker would have said, "all bets are off." See *Ibid*.

[11] Those who hope to have Wm. Shakesphere confirmed as the so-called fifth writer of the Fyre Sygne Thrtre never hesitate to point out that of the many and various spellings of the Bard's name, one or two seem, indeed, to read "Philliamep Shakesfpearfe," or something like it.

the comforting Elizabethan concept of multiple-identity.[12]

Although tradition[13] has at various times attributed a number of the plays of Marlowe, Boone and even Wm. Shakesphere himself[14] to "The Fyre Sygne,"[15] only the aforementioned *Anythynge You Want To* (1605)[16], together with *The*

---

[12] See Carlos Stinken-Boots *The Rise of the Doppleganger in Elizabethan Theatre* in the September 2007 issue of *Digest of Academic Dribble*. Stinken-Boots suggests that Philip Phillip may have been the fourth and fifth Fyre Sygne. He refers to theatre buff and master Northumbrian sorcerer, Alys St. Crowley, who is believed to have conjured up doppelgangers of numerous playwrights of the period. This remarkable trick allowed them to double their output. One of Phillip Phillip's Phillips may have been one of those insubstantial but prolific artists.

[13] As all Firesign scholars learned long ago, Prosper Goncourt has a flippant but understandable way of ascribing *everything* to The Fyre Sygne Thrtre.

[14] See Richard Greene's *A Groatcake of Wits Bought With Millions of Pennys*. Greene often portrayed Robyn Hood in the play *Any Other Part of the Forest* by Lillie and Hellman.

[15] The moniker "Fyre Sygne" reveals the mystical roots of this otherwise rootless band of self-absorbed geniuses. Each was a disciple of one of the four ancient bodies of magical lore. These include the Hermetically Sealed School of Egyptian Geomancy; Master Ki Chain's Glorious Middle Lane; the Celtic Coven of Hynge and Stone; and the brotherhood of Stand-Up Jack and Mason. All of these traditions are subsumed in the synchronic system of the Elizabethan numerologist Robert Fludd. (ee my *The Philosopher's Stone Uncut*, (Korn Circle Press, Antwerp, 2002). Fludd claimed to have discovered the talismanic secret of eternal life, which he lectures on regularly at Dr. Brinkley's Fortnight Medical School in Goatgland, Kansas. Less known, and in many ways his most remarkable achievement, is his deciphering of the Angelic Alphabet. Centuries of Board Certified Charlatans have used Fludd's system to discover divine messages in the most quotidian phrases. Fludd's system is the only tool that reveals the hidden message behind the moniker "Fyre Sygne." The position of the 1st letter in the 1st word is added to itself and added again to the first non-1 in the Fibonacci Series (FS), producing the number 10, which corresponds with "M," the 10th consonant in the Roman Alphabet (RA). Thus "M." The 2nd letter of the 1st word is squared and added to itself, producing the number 4, which corresponds with "O," the 4th member of the Roman Alphabet Vowel Chain (RAVC) a, e, i, o, u. Thus "O." The 3rd letter of the 1st word is squared and added to itself, producing 12, corresponding with "R," the 12th consonant in the RA. Thus "R." The 4th letter of the 1st word retains its original identity, as dictated by *Gedulah*, the fourth flower on the Kaballah's *Sephil Yetzirah* or Tree of Life. *Gedulah* signifies the greatness of self-sustaining identity. (See Rabbi Levi Bootcutt's *Talmudic Topiary of the Tree of Life* (Aleph Press, Buenos Aires, 1934). Thus "E." The 1st position of the 1st letter in the 2nd word are added to produce 3 and doubled as the initial letter of the 2nd word, whose sum is 6, corresponding with 13, the 6th integer in the FS. 13 corresponds with "S," the 13th consonant in the RA. Thus "S." The position of the 2nd letter of the 2nd word is squared and added to itself, producing 5, which corresponds with "U," the fifth member of the RAVC. Thus "U." The sum of the 3rd letter of the 2nd word produces 5, corresponding this time with "G," the 5th consonant of the RA. Thus "G." The 4th letter of the 4th word is subtracted from the letter count of the 2nd word, producing 1, which corresponds with "A," the first member of the RA and the RAVC. Thus "A." The position of the 5th letter in the 2nd word is added to the word's cardinal position and word count, producing 12, corresponding with "R," the 12th consonant in the RA. Thus "R." Replacing "Fyre Sygne" with the letters divined by Fludd's system produces "M O R E S U G A R." This phrase first appears in the Stained Folio of the group's broadside "Ye Straighte Peoples" and signifies either a condemnation of the moral laxity of the times or a yearning for a sweeter, more perfect world. For further confusion see Parcel Moust's *The c6h12o6 Factor in the Fyre Sygne Opus* (*Journal of Critical Chemistry*, Vol. 6) and Rod Wiseacre's *Fyre Sygn As Crypto Peaceniks* (*Minutes of the Colloqium of Fringe Thinking*, 1978). (AS)

[16] However, notoriously grumpy critic Hal Bloom, in a memorable outburst from the classic stage, decried the play as "a palpable forgery!"

*Bummers Playe* (1607)[17], *Devyls Wyves and Saylors Wysdome* (1610)[18] and the tragicomic masque, *The Duke's Delighte*, or *A New Way to Beat Old Debts* (1625)[19] have been positively identified as the work of this mysterious "Fyend-groupe," who "mounted o'er the English backside annoyng all."[20]

*Anythynge You Want To* is, of course, their best-known work — a tribute to the scenery-rending skill "with Tongue and legge"[21] that grants us a few thrilling souvenirs of those heady, bygone days when Good King Jim "rulld ye Sump and brake poore Shakesphere's Pate,"[22] rather than miss a performance at the Fyre Sygne Thrtre.

Set in the miniscule European principality of Pflegm,[23] over which still loom the loamy battlements of the Pflegm Schloss,[24] *Anythynge* has suffered from a

---

[17] Mentioned in *Ye Revelles Booke, Anno 1604*: "On St. Mickees Night, a play of Bummors by Shaxberd, by His Majestys Players."

[18] Recent research has cast doubt on the Fyre Sygne's authorship of this dismal nautical comedy. Pandela Strami's seminal work in bio-reconstructive criticism, *Talk to Me Only With Thy DNA* (Scribbler & Sons, Fresno, 2002) indicts the conventional academic wisdom that ascribes *Devyl's Wyves* to "The Four." Samples of spittle recovered from the play's "Awfull Quarto" (itself recovered from the monastic library of St. Awfull, who was martyred by the critics for being very bad) contain identical DNA to perspiration blotches lifted from the quill of the semi-insane Welsh playwright, Gwylleyn Gynome. Gynome's history as a bum-boy on a series of Her Majesty's "frig-its" qualifies him to recreate the horrendous claustrophobia of the Spanish Stateroom scene, emblematic of the play's unremitting theme of horror and sexual irony.

[19] This last, a *pastiche* of scenes from their earlier work, was first presented after a fifteen-year *caesura* of theatrical activity. Rev. Archie Windsocket of Christschurch University, New Freeland, dubbed this play "either a vain attempt at a comeback or a farewell performance in the manner of Norma Desmond."

[20] Especially *Ibid.*, p. 223.

[21] Ironically *Ibid.*, p. xxi

[22] Emphatically *Ibid.*, p. 375.

[23] Neutral for fifteen hundred years, Pflegm (erroneously, but commonly, spelled "Phlegm") fell victim to the Cold War, and was divided into the Communist Peoples Republic of Plaap Pflegm and the Democratic Oligarchy of Hoch Pflegm. On the Eastern side, the seemingly agricultural Vale of Pflegm was converted into a literal underground beehive of government bureaucracy, known to the KGB as the "Secret People's Bureau of Redundance Bureau." As for the West, the slopes of Mont Pflegm became a sort of glittering safety deposit box for the international jet set. The Democratic Oligarchy grew steadily richer by legalized casino gambling and other up-scale leisure activities. The two halves of Pflegm were dramatically reunited soon after the post-Cold War creation of nearby Servo-Vulgaria, making more practical the long-delayed firing-up of Friendship Stack, a vast atomic power plant which straddles both sides of the former border, the East and West Banks of Rio Pflegmo. (That name, by the way, would seem to be a left-over trace of the brief Spanish Occupation of Pflegm in 1555. King Phyllype marched his gallions back south because they could not hold "ye bunge to ye barrille" after a mere six months in Pflegmland's wettish clime.) See Diswaterer, Albus in *A Rough Guide to Pflegm*, p. 69 (Global Press, Mumbai, 2004)

[24] To historians of The Great War (aka The War To End All Wars) Castle Schloss has a rich and bloody tale to tell. In 1914, when the Kaiser's minions poured into Belgium, a terrible decision was laid across the country's monarch, Bowdown The Third. Mollify the hungry Huns with access to the thousands of Red Cross nurses who had come to the country's aid, or identify a safe haven for the candy stripe corps. It took

surfeit of very bad Folios and, unfortunately, "one two many fulle Quartoes," fermented during the Still Ages of the Puritan Elision.

The plot is told in more-or-less five acts, consisting of mostly interchangeable scenes. What is clear is this: Edmund Edmund, Prince Edmund's illegitimate twin brother, is sent away on a voyage to "Vespucciland," from which he unexpectedly returns, joining forces[25] with the Archbishop of Pflegm as they contrive to wrest control of the land from the Archbishop's brother, the Count-Regent, who has had himself crowned King of Pflegm in the rightful place of his witless nephew (the *soi-dissant* "Clowne Prince[26] Edmund"), who cannot make up his mind about much of anything until he picnics on Marie, his French *cousine*.

Unfortunately, following the burning of the old Fyre Sygne Thrtre by the Puritans in 1642, and despite the subsequent re-restoration of the Fyre Sale Plaehuse in 1766, the original "Fyre Sygne" plays were misplaced, miscopied, garbled, censored and neglected. Only the playwright/plagiarist Colley Cibber ("That weak man,"[27]) somewhat revived one or two in his "laundry" versions of 1801 and 1802. Of the writers themselves, we know only that they disappeared both historically and hystrionically.[28]

Given this sorry demise, productions of *Anythynge* have diverged into the "loose-leaf"

---

three days and hundreds of bottles of Belgium's Lumpen Lager before he reluctantly shipped the sisterhoods of mercy to Castle Schloss, seated deep in the impenetrable Schwartzentote Forest. For two years the nurses discretely worked the platinum mines of the castle's domain. In their spare time they revived the brewing of KOPTGIFT, the region's traditional *aperitif* distilled from absinthe and oak canker. It was this gangrenous liquor that saved the lives, and for some, the virginity of these hard-working sisters. In 1917, a battalion of German *chasseurs* happened across the Castle in retreat before the American Rainbow Division. Drunkards all, the Germans bunged a number of casks of immature KOPTGIFT. The entire battalion went instantly insane and drowned themselves in the Castle's moat as they fled the hydra-headed milkmaid zombies, bent on digesting them, uniforms and all. AS

25 The "forces" envisioned by the Bishop in his famous speech, "Really! My experiments in magnifying pow'r/Do threat to run awry," could be seen to describe a nuclear accident of the Chernobyl variety. A cult has grown up around such "Fyre Sygnes" and other "dangerously oracular" writings, which devotees discover hidden in these muddled texts. In this light, the well-known Hollywood producer and treasure hunter Rick Shakespeare is reportedly preparing a big-budget Hollywood film based on the findings of an undercover journalist at the Flaming Head Oracular Prediction Center (the so-called 'Flamosphere"), near Cummerbund, Arizona.

26 The Fyre Sygne's use of the honorific "Clowne Prince" is received wisdom from a distant past that certainly reached him through the writings of 16th century philatelist Knu Elfcruton. Elfcruton's speculations are copiously referenced in *Karl Jung's Lost Notes* (Parsifal Press, Berne, 1975). Jung's archetypal dream village populated by "originals" disguised as ordinary citizens was ruled by powerful shamans called Clowne Princes. They controlled this unconscious landscape by drug-induced unpredictable behaviour and whacky rhymes and dances that mocked the cultural artifacts that glued the imaginary village together. AS

27 This remark is ascribed to his wife, who is supposed to have then added, "but he is a goode provider." See *Axhandler, Cibber Cybergram* @ oxx.u.com

28 Possibly to the "New Land" of America (called "Vespucciland" by the ever-contrary Pflegmlanders), with its "Red Ingynges and O so savage Breasts that milk a Sages Honey to his Drysing Nees" — words that Proctor Christman himself spoke in the Prologue to *Devyls Wyves*. Another example of "Fyre Sygnes?"

Prompt-Book School[29] and the so-called "Hundred Rewrites" theory (or sect[30]), which attempts to show a "geological" accretion of Ur-Text and Sur-Text over the centuries.

In this edition, we will let the Reader weigh the decision for her or himself, and reproduce the "entire" drama, as dramaturgued by the brilliant 19th century actor-manager known as "The Great Shenannigan"[31] (which was abridged and directed by Derrick Escrow[32] with additional dialogue by Rick Shakespeare[33] for the Prix

---

[29] Prompted by a unique hologram MS in the Oxx. U. Random Access Museum — an actor's "prompt-book," consisting of the first and last words of all his lines and some of his "cue" lines, leaving scholars like ourselves ample room for speculative interpretation.

[30] Joined mostly by academicians of the Boomer counter-culture who "get into" hearing these "texts" read over and over at high speeds, and afterward may have tried anything once. "Art" to these critics is "tantamount to Life." PG

[31] Edwin Shenannigan (1834-1905) was the *pater familias* of this most notable of American theatrical families. His touring productions of *Anythynge, The Mount of County Crisco, The Giant Rat of Sumatra*, and *Brou-ha-ha*, were among the favorites of play-goers in the last century. His sons, Lionel and John sired, between them, three of the great stars of Broadway and film — Ethyl, Reginald and DeSalle. Today, a great-grand-daughter, Drew "Baby" Shenannigan, is a well-known actress, appearing in such films as "Topless" and "The Betty Boop Story." (Edwin is not to be confused with Sir Henry Bloomsday, called, by the Dublin press, "The Great Shenannigan" during his years at the Crabby Theatre.)

[32] ESCROW, DERRICK (January 31, 1945 – ) Australian commercial and film director with music video experience. Born into a middle-class suburb of Melbourne, the son of a bank manager, Escrow opted early for a career in photography. Stressing pride of craftsmanship, he says, "I always liked a well-developed nude." His sense of drama won him many prizes from the Australia-New Zealand Ad Council, and the International "Golden Carrot" at Cannes for his *Breakfast Food Trilogy*, aka "*Pret-a-manger*." The combination of a "romantic setback" and "a taste for adventure" led him to retire in 1975 to a citrus plantation in Corsica, which consumed his time and bankroll. In Pflegm on a commercial shoot in 1980, Escrow was tapped by the National Public Wireless to direct an international cast in *Anythynge You Want To*. The broadcast attracted the attention of the Queen, and HRH attended a morning rehearsal, leaving directly after her *blanc-mange* and turkey roll. Celebrities flocked in her wake to the elegant Palace du Pflegmoisie, which has been meticulously restored by a succession of important trend-setters, only to find Escrow working such acclaimed performers as Lord "Larry" Oliver, Sir "Jack" Feelgood, Dame Tibble Ferndyke, Mickey Rooney, and a very young Kevin Costner (as Second Gravedigger) in the moldy confines of the castle ruins which then overlooked the Texaco Opera House and Petrol Refinery. For more see Zapruder's massive *One Thousand and One Film Directors*, Wakeman House, Rheinstone, NJ, 1988.

[33] Rick Shakespeare is an interesting figure in and of himself. A middle-aged Southern California "importer" and treasure-hunter who reportedly lives on his boat — the "Tem-Pest" — in Retardo Beach, he has been cited in several sensational celebrity scandals in Los Angeles and Las Vegas over the years. He claims to have re-discovered *Anythynge You Want To* in a submerged trunk of his ancestor's belongings, found in a drowned slave vessel off California's Bleak Islands in 1990. The much-trumpeted discovery generated a considerable battle with the United States Department of the Treasury Department, as well as with the Department of Redundancy Department's Un-Lawful Affairs Division. The up-shot is that his claim to be the great-great-great-grand-nephew of Wm Shakespeare has been upheld in some courts (notably the Tribunal of Doctor Me in Tuxedo, Arizona, a privately owned and operated "Supreme" court). It has been often noted that photographs of Rick Shakespeare bear an uncanny resemblance to what few pictures we have of the Bard himself, setting aside the understandable anomaly of the Hawaiian shirts Shakespeare favors. Rick is reported to be a bachelor and to enjoy something called "the fast life." (It is unsure, as we go to press, exactly how fast life is in Southern California at the moment.) DYA

d'Aroma-winning 1981 Raadio Pflegm production, recorded copies of which are available for purchase as you leave the theater. This "most actionable version"[34] concludes with the scandalous burlesque sketch (based on the 18th century *commedia* trope, '*Spera il Conde di Monte Cristo*), which is purported to have been the "only finale possible"[35] originally performed in Elizabethan times.

The sketch, "The Count of Monte Cristo," was reported to have been included in the repertoire of "Dr. Firesign's Antique Theatre of the Plains and Eclectic[36] Buffalo[37] Show" as recently as 1889,[38] thus beginning, or perhaps merely continuing, the theatrical life of this most New World of Elizabethan plays.

---

[34] According to English court records.

[35] Most writers on this subject agree the final act of the celebrated "Shakesphere Revision" — a version in which the old buffoonery has been almost entirely banished — could never have been performed, requiring as it seems to, the anachronous facilities of a large motion-picture company. See Gemstone, *Spielberg or Branagh? That is the Question! The Cinema Heirs of WS*, Solid State University Press, 2004, for a lengthy elaboration of these ideas.

[36] Could this be "Electric?" Chemist Marshal Archer, whose popular Bombaye Opium Restorative and Indian Hell Oil Tonic ultimately lead to the opium-free soft drink known as "Dr Archer," was said to have been a dabbler in "aetheric energy." A useful comparison can be made with the experiences in Treeline, Colorado, of Nicola Teslicle, whose "world stimulator and strapless electric butterfly transmitograph" shocked his contemporaries.

[37] Often spelled "burralo" in early accounts, which has led some researchers to suppose the mascot of the Dr. Firesign company was a jackass instead of a bison. See *Ibid*, if you can find him.

[38] Mentioned but briefly in General Carter's *Western States Journals* for 1906, as part of a report on cattle theft on the Nebraska-South Dakota border. A dramatization by F. Scott Firestone of this quaint epic of America's colorful past was ruthlessly cut from the filmusical *Zachariah, You Crazy Caballero You!* (ABC/Goldfish Pictures, 1970). For more on "The Legend of The Firesign Theatre" consult the Appendices.

# ANYTHYNGE YOU WANT TO
## *Ye Play*

**YE PROLOGUES**

ACT ONE, SCENE ONE
**A SHIP AT SEA**

ACT ONE, SCENE TWO
**THE BLASTED HEATH**

ACT TWO, SCENE ONE
**THE BATTLEMENTS OF CASTLE PFLEGM**

ACT TWO, SCENE TWO
**THE PFLEGMISH COAST**

ACT TWO, SCENE THREE
**THE BISHOP'S CELL**

ACT THREE, SCENE ONE
**THE COUNT'S CLOSET**

ACT THREE, SCENE TWO
**THE GRAVEYARD**

ACT FOUR, SCENE ONE
**THE THRONE ROOM**

ACT FOUR, SCENE TWO
**THE FIELD OF BATTLE**

ACT FIVE, SCENE ONE
**THE BISHOP'S BATTLE TENT**

# YE PLAYERS

**THE COUNT REGENT,** *afterward King of Pflegm*
**ARCHBISHOP OF PFLEGM,** *his brother*
**CLOWN PRINCE EDMUND,** *their nephew, son to the late King Bernardo*
**EDMUND EDMUND,** *bastard son to the late King*
**SWEET MARIE,** *couisine to Edmund and the Bishop's ward*[39]
**STORMENDRANG, HAPPENSTANCE, FANGBONER,** *courtiers*
**CHEVALIER PIERRE DE CARDENTTE,** *a couturier*
**PETE OF PIKE, GRAPESHOT, MUZZLE,** *Men-at-arms*
**SIR ANDREW LUNCH,** *a Scottish knight*
**HOLE and MOLE,** *gravediggers*
**FLOUNDER,** *a Pflegmish beachcomber*
**MARINARA,** *an accountant*
**PESTIO,** *a clown*
**BO SUN,** *A Japanese Pirate*
**EARL OF MULHOLLAND,** *a Highlands nobleman*
**BARON FAIRFAX,** *Provisioner-Royal*
**MAYOR OF BURBANK,** *an honorary Gentleman*
**ARGYLE, BEVERLY, MELROSE,** *Pflegmish Lords*
**THREE WEIRD COOKES**
**THE PROLOGUE**
**ISIS,** *A Dancing Girl*[40]
**A DUMB SHOW:** *Rustick Players, Maidens, Fooles, Twits, Squirrelles*[41]

---

[39] These five players may be considered the central figures of the traditional *commedia* performed at fairs in the countryside around Milan which, according to Edwin "The Great" Shenannigan, inspired (along with a history of Pflemland titled *Voyages Among the Flegm Landers, and a Chronicale of their Vyle Pyrate Kings*, circulating in Europe in the mid-16th century) Shakesphere's play. For more about *il Conde, il Cardinale, Edmundo, Gemello,* and *Dolce Maria,* see the notes for '*Spera il Conde di Monte Cristo.*

[40] Unknown in Shakesphere's time where Shakespheare lived (though a popular palace attendant in the Middle East), the dancing girl was created for the Escrow Raadio Pflegm production, where she was played by a Foley sound effect.

[41] This Dumb Show, which looks like it must have been a lot of fun, was an "opener" at the Globe Theatre. There was, of course, no text, and no player ever wrote down what the Twits and Squirrels were doing, so the point of it is lost in the sands of mime.

*"While on your arses, warming up your seats,
Admit me Prologue to this dreadful piece!"*
Sir Jack Feelgood in the 1972 musical version, "Anythynge!"

# ANYTHYNGE YOU WANT TO

## The Prologue

*An Overture: Sackbuttes, Goatpipes and Tambor*

*ENTER THE BISHOP, sinisterly, from the Left Aras*

**BISHOP:** Come Clownmen, Slackers, Seekers all!
Is there seat unfill'd in this most crowded hall?
You, Jack the 'Prentice with his scul'ry Nell[42]
And Will the Groomsman close by sultry Belle,

*A DUMB-SHOW is enacted. Two Brothers kill'd and Nuncles wroth. Ghosts and Witches. Twits and Squirrles.*

Behold! Two brothers, both alike, yet never met,[43]
In far-off Pflegmland, where our scene is set.

One, from New World pleasures doth come back,
Yet hurricanes apart his noble ship doth crack.
The other, somewhat gone with cakes and ale,

---

[42] "Nell" is short for "Orange Nell," a saucy wench who was actually a man (Geoffrey Clapper) who revolutionized the look of Shakespeare's women by secreting Spanish oranges in his doublet to simulate breasts. He gave new dimensions to his portrayal of the Floating Ophelia and the "ill-starred" Caesar — nicknamed "Orange Julius." Clapper was rumored to have been the Bard's main squeeze.

[43] The 1847 "Weirdly School" MS, found in the Max Cool Library Extended Collection has a "Chorus" intone a Prologue for performances by "youngsters and simpletons":
    In Phlegmish times, two warring houses
    Did unite in happy strife, one 'pon the nother
    And brother fought with brother, sore with pride, inside,
    Inside the dismal castle walls
    Where still a dark and aweful secret hangs
    Between a Count and his confused clan,
    Made more confus'd by midnight ming'ling 'twixt ancestral sheets!
    Yet all that's dark and weird at dawn
    Shall be illumined by the rightful son
    And come to swift conclusion when the day is done.
    Now, pray, our dearth of lights and set you not resent,
    As this, our tragic play of happy mirth we doth present.

Espys his royal father's spectre pale.

Both are but the tools of foolish Nuncles' greed,
Each of whom would sieze the throne and lead
Old Pflegmland down some rocky road.

The rapid[44] passage of their comic schemes
Is now the awful traffic of our shaggy joke,
The which, if you attend, like unto dreams,
Swift will vanish, like so much hempish smoke.[45]

---

[44] One of the most debated words in the Shakesphere canon, it appears differently spelled in all but two of the contemporary printings. Folio Oxx 4, has "rabid," Oxx 5 (The Incomplete Folio of 1605) has "rabbit," and the First Full Quarto has (of all things), "wrap it." The Great Shenannigan also considered "raped" and "rarebit" before deciding on what he considered the obvious.

[45] This rude and unsubtle ur-Prolog, pandering to the rowdies "i' the pit," must have preceded by twenty years the following magisterial evocation attributed to a re-writing by Wm. Shakespheare, "after a Fifth of Old Harry."

PROLOGUE:    O for a microphone and wire, that would disturb
             Electric wave and mount the aether's firey tide
             To batter up 'gainst list'ner's playful ears!
             Come Janus, double-visag'd god of Grants!*
             Let loose the gravy-suck'ling dogs to nurse
             The swelling governmental Teat.
             Like ancient Rome and Uncle Remulus,
             The nutur'd pups would be endow'd with pow'r enough
             To Howl their artful message up to
             Yonder dish-faced Moon, and track their Milky Way
             Around the Dawn-link'd, all-connected Globe.
             Imagine then how tongues would wag, what tails they'd tell!
             Had we but ears for such a pitch, 'twould give us paws
             Or make us flee, as Hellhounds after Styx!
             Why wait? Because we've not been check'd?**
             Can we be cancell'd on our writeful stamping ground?
             Are we on Hold? Say nay!***
             We'll tell the story loud, and teach,
             By stretching taut a string from can****
             To Canterbury, thence to Cannes in France
             And e'en on to Canton Town, where it shall pass
             Through chinks in Cathay's awesome Wall!
             Well, well . . . Here goes!

---

\* Some versions read "grass." Is the speaker begging Good King James for money in this passage? It would seem so. Raleigh relates asking the Queen for a shipment of Gold to "Prime ye pumpe."

\*\* It has often been noted that much of this prologue seems to foretell the advent of electricity and other scientific wonders certainly unknown to the authors. But what are we to make of the American spelling? There was not much of a banking system in 1605. You had to fight for your money. Christofer Shakespeare was himself wounded by a large Gouda Cheese during a rapier duel over an ill-calculated royalty payment. It would seem the author (or authors) signal us that though they've not the means to

*Lerndon 1610 B Litz fecit*

make their visions real, yet they will by primitive means make their story heard clear to China. (China had but recently been discovered, somewhere "beyond Leeds.") Was this play written in the Americas? It seems so, certainly. But did the author go there? That is the question. Or was the author an early resident, even? (There is another question, but it cannot be dealt with here.) D.Y.A. {H. Bloom calls it "a palpable phony" ED)

\*\*\* This matches the account in Raleigh's Journal that there was some delay before a "Shippe of Monies" reached them."

\*\*\*\* A string *was* stretched between the spire of Canterbury Cathedral and the Chapel of St. Tintin in Cannes in 1599, although its use was not understood at the time. Could a string have been strung as well from Virginia across the Atlantic to Canterbury? It seems unlikely. It would have had to have been a very long string.

# ANYTHYNGE YOU WANT TO
## *THE PROLOGUE, TAKE TWO*[46]

*An Overture: Gazatchorns, Slack Key Viol, Nose-honker*

ENTER THE COMPANY *as their Characters in the Comedia*[47]

**EDMUNDO:** Come Clownmen, Slackers, Seekers all!
Sits seat unfill'd in this most crowded hall?[48]

**CONDE:** You, Jack the 'Prentice with his scull'ry Nell
And Will the Groomsman close by sultry Belle![49]

**ED DUO:** Rude gentles all, slipped here, into our privy Pit
To view this half-day's Progress of our most aweful wit!

**CARDINALE:** While on your arses, warming up your seats,
Admit us Prologue to this dreadful piece.

**EDMUNDO:** And find no cause to leave
For doors are locked behind thine unsuspecting feets.

*A DUMB SHOW ACCOMPANIED BY MUSICK*

*EDMUND WALKS DRINKING READING A BOOK,*
*EDMUND EDMUND SWIMS FOR HIS VERY LIFE*

---

[46] This playful Prologue is thought to have been devised by Phillip Philip for a Royal Entertainment in 1610. It was often revised by members of Ye Fyre Signe, depending on whose turn it was to speak the lines.

[47] Another, recently discovered, "side" gives all these lines to the Bishop, who enters "sinisterly left, from an arass." Christies, Celebrity Antiques Sale Catalog, April 1996.

[48] The traditional opening of a Milanese *commedia*, following three nose-honker blasts.

[49] Rick Shakespeare claims to have found the "politicallie correcte" translation of these lines: "You, Jack the Lawyer, briefing scull'ry Nells/And Bill the Gamester ring'd by sul'try Belles."

| | |
|---|---|
| **CONDE:** | Behold! Two brothers, twins! Yet never met, <br> In far-off Pflegmland, where our sober scene is set. |
| **CARDINALE:** | One, from New World pleasures hurries back, <br> While hurricanes his over-laden barque doth crack. |
| **CONDE:** | The other, brainpan flushed and stout with ale, <br> Espys his royal father's fearsome spectre pale. |

*THE DUMB SHOW CONTINUES WITH IL CONDE SPOOKING EDMUND AND IL CARDINALE STEWING UP A WITCHES BREW*

| | |
|---|---|
| **EDMUNDO:** | Both twins the tools of foolish Nuncles' greed. |
| **ED ED:** | As Greybeard plots to seize the crown — |
| **EDMUNDO:** | Baldly[50] dreams to melt Our Pflegmland down <br> And lead poor Pflegmland down a rocky road! |
| **ED ED:** | Through less than tasty courses, lac'd with toad. |

*THE DUMB SHOW CONTINUES WITH SEVERAL SWORDFIGHTS, A DEATH BY POISON, ETC.*

| | |
|---|---|
| **CARDINALE:** | The vapid[51] passage of their misplaced schemes <br> Is now the nawful traffic of our shaggy joke.[52] |
| **CONDE:** | The which, if you attend, like unto dreams, <br> Swift will vanish, like so much hempish smoke.[53] |
| **EDMUNDO:** | Yet, if wouldst be pilot of our leaky ship, <br> But touch thy finger to 'lectronic chip.[54] |

---

[50] The *Cardinale* is traditionally costumed with a bald-pate.

[51] "Torpid?"

[52] "Shaggy," from Old High Phlegm — "shagged," meaning falsely baited.

[53] Hemp rope was an Elizabethan stage-manager's prop — burned backstage to produce a dense fog, such as the one in Act 1, Sc. 2.

[54] These and the following lines were added to explain the "Interactive" production of AYWT mounted during the 1995 Pflegmish Pfisstival of the Pfarts.

| | |
|---|---|
| **ED ED:** | We'll do our best to satisfy your Choyce<br>With nimble Wit and minimum of Noyse. |
| **CONDE:** | Still all, to pay the mounting bills when they come due,<br>We Mountebanks will strive in spite of Will — |
| **EDMUNDO:** | To earn your dread acclaim and thus your hand — |
| **ED ED:** | By doing that, which thou dost us command. |
| **BISHOP:** | Or, in a word, we'll try our best to do — |
| **ALL:** | Anythynge You Want Us To! |

*EXEUNT OMNES*

*"What brouhaha! What haps, sweet chaps?"*
*Buster Artunian as Happenstance in Blanque Cheque's*
*1975 production at the Theatre-in-the-Garage*

# ANYTHYNGE YOU WANT TO
## ACTE ONE, SCENE ONE[55]

*A Ship at Sea. Thunder Clapps.*[56]

*ENTER Sailors upon the pitching Deck.*

**BOSUN**[57]: Storm ho!

**SAILOR 2:** A tempest yares[58] across the sea!

**SAILOR 3:** Lightning starboard[59] boils the sea!

---

55 Orson Welles, for his 1936 Mercurial Theatre CBS radio production (in which he played both Edmund and Edmund Edmund), brilliantly intercut between this dark and stormy scene and Scene Two in which he cast the Weird Cooks as Haitian witch doctors.

56 Nowhere is the Fyre Sygne's prescience better demonstrated than in this scene upon the sea. The entire scene is a prognostication of the Spanish Armada's destruction by "wylde gayles" in the English Channel in 1588. Edmund Edmund is certainly the inspiration of the Sygne's Philip Phillip. An obvious reference to Philip II, the King of Spain who sent his multitude of war ships to invade England in order, as Edmund Edmund declares, "to set that privy throne upon my head." The ship in which Edmund Edmund travels (a symbol of the Armada) is paid for by the spoils of Spain's North American empire, here described as the "Broad leaf'd land of mighty Roi-Tan." The ship is peopled with fops and defeatist seamen who know "all's lost, we're doomed." There is no logical explanation for the playwrights' uncanny ability to predict the future. Some critics like Darrell Fratpants in his *A Repudiation of Everything I Don't Understand* claims that the play was obviously written after 1588 and that the authors used the failed invasion as an inspiration for this scene. This is palpably absurd, as two of the Fyre Sygnes set sail for the New World in 1585 — see my *English Seed And Iroquois Corn* (Washon Press, Toledo, 1999). AS

57 Some scholars, finding this character's name also printed "Bo Sun," have speculated that the craft may have been manned by Asian pirates. This view is supported by the later reference to one of the hexagrams of the *I Ching*. Indeed, in the "hopelessly corrupt" (Cambridge Editors) MS "P", the Bosun's lines are given to one "Capt. Jingge." Some alternate readings from this draft, which Warburton and Malone assign to a traveling "reduced" Fyre Sygne company, are noted as "P" below.

58 Veers. This "tempest" was clearly inspired by the Great Hoch Pflegm Hurricane of 1599, after which, miles of coastline, sand and shingle, were covered in tar — the cargo of a fleet of French men-o-war returning from siphoning the oil seeps in the Gulf of St. Louis for material to caulk the ships' seams.

59 The side of the ship that the stars are on.

**SAILOR 4:** Look, Pilot, at the darkening of the light![60]

**BOSUN:** The moon seems drown'd in rain![61]

**SAILOR 2:** All's wet!

**SAILOR 3:** All's lost!

**SAILOR 4:** Let's split![62]

**BOSUN:** Let's not split yet! Stand ye pat!
All hearts above!
A shuffling fate cuts not this deck!
Come Jacks! Lay down your hands and pull!
Pull to the straight![63]
By deuce, we'll not be Neptune's guests[64] tonight!

Pull! Pull!

**SAILORS:** Yare! Yare! Yare . . .

*Exeunt Sailors. ENTER two Courtiers.*[65]

**STORM:** What bruhaha![66] What haps, sweet chaps?
The rocking boat hath rolled you out of bed,
I fear. Come Dirk! Come Kink![67]

---

[60] Hexagram 36 — Ming I. The Judgment is, "In adversity it furthers one to be persevering."

[61] Another conclusive indication of the Eastern influence on this scene: these two lines form a perfect haiku.

[62] A reference to the common Elizabethan disease of multiple identity.

[63] Perhaps this was a "tong" or Chinese gambling vessel? See Alien, Patricia, *From Hopeless Bay to Cape Absurd: Noodling Among the China Isles* (reprinted by Sound Books, WV 1992).

[64] See *Michelin Guide to Norwegian Waters*, p. 42.

[65] The English playwright Sam Shopphard brought these cardboard characters vividly to life in his 1964 drama, *Stormendrang and Happenstance Are Gay*.

[66] Noise. From the Old French "brou Nana," meaning "mother's milk." This common expression was, however, excised from many performances, due to the tendency of the groundlings to cry "Ha ha ha, ha ha ha ha!" in response, thus stopping the performance in its tracks.

[67] These are common names for "iffemynit ladds," which were a common feature of Elizabethan Masques.

Come first mates back!
And tie me to the mast face front,
E'er I in this gale's storm[68] be lost!

**HAPPEN:** Oh! Oh!

*He Pukes[69] upon the Groundlings.*

**STORM:** Heigh ho, good Signor Happenstance!
What drives thee 'pon the poop[70]
This dreadful day?

**HAPPEN:** My stomach's gone off-course again, I fear.
There's naught to eat aboard but souvenirs[71]
From exiled Edmund Edmund's Indian land.

**STORM:** What? Liked thee not the smoking fowled Stew?[72]
Tabac and Turkey, two New World wonders, these!

**HAPPEN:** They're strangely met, friend Stormendrang.
That red-necked duck[73] was never meant
To sailor be . . . Ahg . . .

*Again, he Pukes.*

---

[68] Gale Storm, the film and radio actress, took her name from this line. See Flack, Leonard, *Gale! What A Gal!* (Celebrity Press, Hollywood CA, 1992)

[69] Heaves. Blows chunks.

[70] Normally, the "head" or "can" would be located on this deck.

[71] So word had reached "Lerndon" as early as 1605, that the Native Americans had much to offer Pflegmish traders. The Pflemlanders, however, seemed unable to interpret the differing instructions for "smoking" the wondrous, but unfamiliar birds and plants from their New Pflegmland Colony, briefly located downwind of present-day Winston-Salem, S. C. (Later, in Act 2, Scene 1, we will discover another important New World import, crude oil.) See Appendix.

[72] This seems similar to the recipe published by Chef Crockette as "Burnt Turkoman Stuft mit Havana" in *The Edible Shakespeare*, Thos. Cooke & Sons, Lerndon, 1934. The famously "corrupt" MS "P" has it as "twyce ympressed duck," leading to the Chef's "King Duck," served before many crowned heads-in-exile in the Chef's swank Melody Room in London's fashionable Upping Square.

[73] Such was the stupidity of the early New World colonials (known as red-necks to the local Native Americans), that they assumed the turkey (*wattlewattle holidi*) to be a kind of land-bound duck, which they were exceedingly thankful they could catch.)

**BOSUN** [*OFF*]: Duck below! Duck! Duck![74]

**STORM:** Yet how it sails! Come back below,
O bilious Happenstance, O hallow'd Happenstance!

**HAPPEN:** Now, hollow'd Happenstance!

**STORM:** But stay! For Edmund Edmund[75] storms up from below!

*ENTER EDMUND EDMUND, Drunk.*

**ED ED:** Halloo![76] Halloo![77] Where's everyone?[78]
Ah, Stormendrang!
I've sunk the Captain with my sack and told
But half my tale. 'Twas thus I left it off —
"All the Shores were Glitch'd and Gloomy,[79]
Broad-leaf'd Land of mighty Roi-Tan.[80]
Little White Owl, drew I her to me,
Injuns watching, wooden, dead-pan . . ."[81]

*Pitch'd from his feet, Edmund Edmund falls Below.*

---

74 "Thrice-ympressed?" Another Asian reference!

75 Not the first appearance by this mysterious figure of Elizabethan lore. He is mentioned in Sydney's *New Worldes Loste* and in Roan and Martyn's *Ye Laffe Inne*. Since his two names are interchangeable, it is unknown which is the first and which the patronymic. He is a figure of fun, a "self-referential man," as e. e. cummings was remarked to have remarked.

76 Hello.

77 Hi!

78 Offstage, evidently.

79 This lay would seem to be the repeat of what Edmund Edmund later recites before the Count in Act 4, Sc. i, and was as well the obscured signal for an explosive event. Guy Ffawlkes was known to have set up as a signal for the explosion under the Houses of Parliament the words "Glitched and Gloomy," though they were eventually misinterpreted by the conspirators.

80 Should this not be Roatan? Or might it not refer to the "Dark" or "Dusky King" — a legendary hero of Pflegmish folklore?

81 The relentless trochees of Edmund Edmund's narrative, which evoke the simple rhythms of Iroquois "warriors with their plumes and war-clubs," were once familiar to all American children, forced to memorize D. H. Longfellow's immortal poem, "Gitchee-Goomee."

| | |
|---|---|
| **HAPPEN:** | Hear how our Master Edmund Edmund is<br>Near drown'd with drink![82] |
| **STORM:** | Thy greenish cast hath spoiled his anecdote<br>Of Victory o'er the hapless Iroquois.[83] |
| **HAPPEN:** | Full twenty times I've heard him pick<br>That bloody-nosed fight and win!<br>Thanks giving we should get, for from the<br>Feathered horde we pluck'd him hence! |
| **STORM:** | I would this mission done, and we were dock'd<br>On Pflegmland's wealthy banks, and I at home,<br>In bed. |
| **HAPPEN:** | You'll sleep in bed, with Ned,[84] when our<br>Explosive charge is safe delivered to<br>The Bishop's churchy seat.[85] |
| **STORM:** | But hush, look out. He comes anon. |
| **ED ED:** | "Spirits toughened by Dutch Masters,[86]<br>Left I White Owl, Christen'd Muriel,[87] |

---

[82] To which Storm. replies (in the "P" ms), "I fear our host, the Chinese Captain, cannot understand a word he says."

[83] A Native American confederation of the upper Ohio River and its various drainages. It is doubtful that there was any victory over them, as they were all-powerful at this time. See Armstrong-Anderson's *Military Victories and Armaments of Savages*, London, 1943. "Parmisans" in the MS "P."

[84] Sorry for the interruption, but isn't this the same Ned that Edmund mourns? Either they are ignorant of their companion's untimely demise, a victim of the Black Plague (see II, iv), or is this a masked reference to their ultimate fate?

[85] A clear reference to the "Eleven Piles of Luther" which were nailed to the crescent-mooned door of the Abbey of Lithium in 1603.

[86] These, the Elders of Ghont, supposedly visited by the historical Edmund Edmundo in his semi-mythical journey, "The Friesland Saga" of 1589, were professors of 'Pataphysics and Ariel Philosophy at Hoch Pflegm Gymnasium.

[87] Actually Old French "Mur reel," or "What a wall!" — a common expression among French friars when dipping a well-endowed savage sweetie into a lake. A contemporary equivalent would be "Built like a brick outhouse." See Peter Savatte, *The Naughty Wordbook*, Solid State Press, 1984.

                'Stead of siring[88] New World bastards,
                Gave my head to schemes Impurial!"
                'Znuts![89] What's happen'd to our
                Righteous speed?[90]
                Who slipped the shrouds and loos'd
                The hempen jute?[91] Hath courage run aground?

**STORM:** Twice noble friend, I fear a storm
Is blowing up our aft.[92]

**ED ED:** Good gushing Stormendrain, of blanc-mange[93]
Face, must warlike virtue jell before this
Quaking gale?
What pudding-liver'd custard trifles
With our Holy Junket[94] home to Pflegm[95]?

**HAPPEN:** Bring not up food, my Prince, or I shall
Follow suit toute suite upon thy suit, I fear.

**ED ED:** O purged Happenstance, this freakish wind
Will blow us naught but good!
Saw not the mast! Cut not the wind,
Nor throw those barrels o'er!

---

**88** Edmund Edmund evidently gave up his usual philandering pursuits in the New World. This was not unusual, as sexual disease was rampant. ("Rampants," by the way, were the blousey drawers worn by randy gentlemen of the day.)

**89** God's nuts, or God's bounty. See Blake.

**90** There was a potion called "righteous speed" which was said to have fueled the exploits of Lucifer's Angels, a "wheeled fynd grup" reported ranging the moors of Staffordshire in 1541. Also called the "Beast of Debtford."

**91** References to "ye hemppe" are numerous in Shakesphere's body of work. See notes re "Ye Mystic Hams" and "Sacred Pot."

**92** Rear. The ms "P," which no less a scholar than Luther attributed to "an Eastern man, with naught but theft upon his mind," has "Capt. Jing" entering and laying about with such orders as "Decrease sails! No starch in sheets!" and "Roll out barrels!"

**93** A French expression. See Sir Montley Pythion's "Le Tennise des Scottische" (1610).

**94** These were paid pilgrimages. Edmund Edmund and his allies "wood hav stayed in the Bar-Mouthes." See Fangboner, Charlie, *Bar-Mouthes Hopping on the Spanish Maine.* Black Water Press, Tortuga, 1924.

**95** Note several references in this speech to popular London desserts, most of them still popular, which says a lot about English cuisine.

| | |
|---|---|
| **STORM:** | Those barrels? Our servants lie within those barrels![96] |
| **ED ED:** | And all the others fill'd with light, sweet crude.[97] |

*Thunder Clapps.*

| | |
|---|---|
| **BOSUN [OFF]:** | Again the storm! |
| **STORM:** | A cloud! |
| **HAPPEN:** | Give up! |
| **BOSUN [OFF]:** | To foc'sle[98] go ye down! |
| **ED ED:** | Go down?<br>Not down, nor out! But home at last<br>To turgid Pflegm![99]<br>My Nuncle Bishop prays and pays<br>For my unknown return.<br>Five golden Crowns for each of ye who stays!<br>But only one for me. Just one. |
| **ALL:** | But one? |
| **ED ED:** | One is enough, when it's the Holey Crown.<br>Our rever'd Hat.[100] Our homely, down-turn'd Bowl,<br>O'er-rimm'd with ancient fur<br>And flush'd with pride. |

---

[96] These natives, smuggled aboard for what may have been immoral and/or domestic reasons, were undoubtedly Pflegmland's first illegal aliens.

[97] Edmund Edmund's reference here to "crude" oil or asphaltum has an alchemical connection to the Bishop's experiments. A valuable commodity, however environmentally toxic, it was to be Edmund Edmund's "ticket home."

[98] The place in a ship where the foc'ing normally happens. The joke is painfully drawn out.

[99] Of the well-known features of Pflegmland in the 16th century, the most often mentioned were its boiling hot summer storms. Also "turdid" in the aptly-named "polluted" Folio.

[100] The Crown of Pflegmland is none of these, of course. The Author or Authors are evidently referring to the English Crown.

> Our country's awe-ful Lid, its Sacred Pot.[101]
> I'll set that privy throne upon my head
> Though Nature force me circumgate the Globe!
> Sit out this storm? Nay! Lay on sheets!
> Then crack cracked cheeks and break, wind,
> Loudly break![102] Bend backs and buttocks, boys!
> Twill be a piece of cake!

**BOSUN:** Yare! She's breaking up!

**HAPPEN:** We drown!

**ALL:** We're doomed![103]

*Amid Thunder Clapps, EXEUNT OMNES.*

*A Royal MUSICK.*

---

[101] "Pot," or *cannabis sativa*, has been held "sacred" in many cultures. Unknown in Europe at this time, along with corn, tomatoes and chocolate, it may have been mixed with this first shipment of Indian Tobacco, thus adding to the confusion.

[102] All too redolent of Shakespeare's words in *King Leer*.

[103] The final lines of the "magnificently corrupt" Magnum Quarto have been taken by some (see Reinshriber, *Shakespeare Wrote Shakespheare*) as proof that Wm. Shakesphere was the true author of at least four of Shakespeare's plays.

**ED ED:** This wind can blow us naught but good.
Fold not the mast! Put on more sail!

**CPT JING:** Much ado about nothing!
Happen every Twelfth Night!
Go way!

**ED ED:** Go away? Where? Where do we go,
But home to Pflegm?
My Nuncle Bishop prays and pays for my return.
Sit out this storm? Nay!
A great white sail is what we need to clear the decks
For what's in store to be our lot.

*The Great Oil Spill of 1599. Section of Mural at the Pflegmish Embassy, Washington, DC.*

**CPT JING:** As you like it. Anything you want to.
Or, Whatever!

**ED ED:** Now, crack cheeks and break wind, break!
We'll die at sea or live on land
For History's sake!

*"These great conundrums fit me not."*
*Antonio Shortears as The Bishop.*
*Plastic Armour Theatre production at The Ash Globe (1972).*

# ANYTHYNGE YOU WANT TO
## ACTE ONE, SCENE TWO

A Nawful Place, upon the heath at dawn.

THUNDER CLAPPS. MOANING of a doodlesack.

BUBBLING of the Pot.

ENTER Three Weird Cookes,[104] each spoiling the Broth.[105]

**1ST COOK:**   Come cooking cousins, stoke the peat!
Boil the oil and beat the meat![106]

---

[104] The "thre wyrd Cookes" are all too reminiscent, of course, of the three Witches in Shakespheare's *Macheath*. As well as those, they stir a pot and live on prophesy. These are often mentioned as arguments that William Shakespeare himself is the so-called "Fifth Author" of Ye Fyre Sygne Thrtre.

[105] The presence of three witches, not five, in this scene is further proof of the Fyre Sygne's deep roots in the occult. There is hardly a medieval play ("The Coven Dyscovered," "Maudie Maggot Vomits Up The Wee One") or an example of Elizabethan drama ("Shoes For The Cauldron's Feet," "The Hagge That Wound Nay Floate") in which the coven is composed of more or less than five witches. Each of the five represents one of the traditional humors – choler, melancholy, black and yellow bile and phlegm. The authors have reduced the coven to three, with each witch representing one of the three humors that underlie a more ancient and esoteric tradition. They are Kapsicum, Disturbia and Hochlugee. Kapsicum is the humor of energetic self-destruction. Disturbia is the humor of creative self-loathing. Hochlugee is the humor of mordant self-projection. The progenitor of this tripartite explanation of the human condition was a secret society formed in Periclean Greece named The Brotherhood of Kappa Delta. Kappa for Kapsicum and Delta for Disturbia. There is no Greek letter "H." To remain underground, The Brotherhood constructed their European headquarters by tunneling grottos beneath the cathedrals at Chartres, Mont St. Michael, Canterbury and The Vatican's St. Paul's. For eight centuries the Kappa Deltas thrived until they were unearthed by The Grand Guild of Masons. The Masons stoned the vast majority of the Brotherhood to death for compromising the architectural integrity of the magnificent edifices they had fashioned over the centuries. Remnants of the Kappa Delta subterranean tombs remain, each bearing an identical symbol over the entrance — a pepper and a 'pothecary pill resplendent on a three-petaled rosette. On closer scrutiny the rosette reveals itself as a crenellated wad of mucous. AS

[106] Meat was often crushed between pestles at the time to make it "tendre." Also, it was a common practice to use mutton or venison as drums.

| | |
|---|---|
| 2ND COOK: | I've deep-fried fowl,[107] a bucket-load![108] |
| 3RD COOK: | This fowl is fair![109] |
| 2ND COOK: | It's laced with toad! |
| 1ST COOK: | This oil is black as fish-folk's gloom. |
| 2ND COOK: | Here's clams and oysters — |
| 1ST COOK: | They've met their doom! |
| 3RD COOK: | Add spleen of banker, hand of cop,[110] Tongue of lawyer, dearly bought! |
| 2ND COOK: | Wing of condor, whoop of crane, Dolphin's throat and sperm-whale's brain! |
| 1ST COOK: | I've whooping cough! |
| 2ND COOK: | And filthy eggs! |
| 3RD COOK: | Crawly bed bugs! |
| 2ND COOK: | Just their legs! |
| 1ST COOK: | Devil'd bees! |
| 2ND COOK: | And firey ants! |

---

[107] A reference to the common Chikene-Standes that overran London in the years between 1601 and 1620. They were eventually outlawed by the Lord Chamberlain. NB: Some versions say "spott'd owl." The Folger Folio, on view in Washington, D. C. has the curious couplet: "Of mouth of Newt, a caucus-load./ This Newt is foul, it looks like Toad." Similarly, the National Library's copy offers, "From mouth of Newt a load of dung!/St. Sara's bile!/O'Donnel's lung." St. Sara of Wasilla was boiled in bile for false piety; newts are small creatures given to a reverse digestive process; "Paddy" O'Donnell was a notorious loudmouth in the Irish parliament.

[108] Attributed to a Colonel Pulliet of the Virginia Colony of 1605. A "buck'tt load" in the colonies was what could be carried by a buck, or Indian male. (Another telling New World reference.)

[109] Also, "with secret sauce," explained by Chef Crockette as "salt, sugar and pickles."

[110] A hand which poaches, "robs Peter to pay Peter," (John Donne, *The Loveres Till*, 1587). Later, someone who destroys or alters evidence of a crime.

**3RD COOK:** Here's Lady Gaga's old meat pants![111]

**1ST COOK:** All must seethe and boil like lava
While we take Five[112] for mocha-java![113]

*They Laugh and Gossip. A Thunder Clapp.*

*ENTER THE COUNT-REGENT and THE BISHOP OF PFLEGM, Riding.*[114]

**BISHOP:** Come dozy[115] brother, slug-abed, keep up!
Thy pace, snail-darter-like, doth drive me mad![116]
These hags stay op'ned not much after dawn.
Lord Michelin[117] says the vision in their pot
Goes stale by ten.

**COUNT:** But Bishop brother,
You drag me drugged from my
Dream-drench'd Couch,
Ere Morphine's[118] fingers loose their loving grasp.

---

111 These seven lines were graphically presented in J. Goodman's printing of 1700, apparently taken from a Grande Guignol production of the play at the Theatre Royal, from which H. R. H. quickly departed during this scene. Lord and Lady Gaga of Brest were eaten by ants on their expedition to South Wales in 1698.

112 Believed to refer to the five musicians who played at the Theatre. There is extant a reference to "Take Ye A Fiver" as a hymn written by Desmond Brew-back, who was known to have played the bag-stoat in the Globe's "Smalle Consort," which provided music in the pit.

113 A potent mixture of chocolate, black pepper and gin-sing root, served as a beverage at Ye Latte Hus, a Cheapside drinking establishment.

114 This must have been a spectacular entrance in the 19th century "Wild West" version, but in Victorian times naked animals, especially "equines, studs and asses" were banned from public display, being reserved exclusively for private "consorts" with the Queen. The mounts were feigned.

115 Sleepy.

116 Make me crazy.

117 Lord Michelin, a disinherited, spoiled dandy of the court, who tirelessly passed his days shamelessly sponging off the owners of inns, taverns, brothels, hustleries, castles and estates, justifying his wastrel existence by publicly posting his personal critiques, which were predictably positive unless he was "barred entrance or rudely serv'd."

118 The twin Greek Olympians, Morphina, goddess of dreams and procrastination. Morphinus was the god of Neuron receptors. (See "Endorphine's Plaint" by John Lilly.)

|  |  |
|---|---|
|  | And all for what? To feed me fancies<br>From a gypsy stew?[119]<br>Better we should stay abed and pray. |
| **BISHOP:** | Stay sweet'n'low,[120] my dulcy bro'.<br>Our Kingless country, perch'd on civil war,<br>Commands us leg it here[121] to pagan heath,<br>And lend an ear to mouths of prophecy. |

*A Thunder Clapp. Moan of Doodlesack.*[122]

*The Three Weird Cookes appear.*

|  |  |
|---|---|
| **BISHOP:** | Hags and cronies! What's thy spell? |
| **1ST COOK:** | It's simple, sire — |
| **2ND COOK:** | Don't ask! |
| **3RD COOK:** | Don't tell![123] |
| **1ST COOK:** | Hail Bane of Pflegm! Noble Regent!<br>Weighty Count! |
| **2ND COOK:** | Hail Feign of Grunge![124] Keeper of our p'lutted heir! |
| **3RD COOK:** | Hail, canny Count, that after death shall rise<br>A King! |

---

[119] Hemlock Stones, the illustrious fictional detective, is known to have written a monograph titled "Gypsies of Pflegmland and the Nethers," researched during his long "exile" as a violence student among Themselves, as the Gypsies call themselves. Chef Crockette, *ibid*, gives an interesting recipe for "Mrs. Murphy's Genuine Gypsy Stew," which includes the morphine.

[120] Silent.

[121] Ankle to dailies.

[122] A medieval musical instrument which had two or three roosters stuffed into an inflated leather pouch, and which was played with the feet. The result was deafening.

[123] "Non curio, non dicto" was the illiterate motto of the Royal House of Pflegm.

[124] The "Sacred and Olde Order of Feign" was an antique Scottish noble title. Grunge was a Highland district near Pendelton where men wore their heavy shirts tied around their waists.

**COUNT:** [ASIDE] I like the taste of this!

**BISHOP:** What, hateful hags — no hail for me?

**1ST COOK:** No hail for thee, for thou shall never reign!

**2ND COOK:** Thy Bishoprick is circumscribed![125]

**3RD COOK:** Thy cocky plans fall short!
Thou'lt ne'er be satisfied!

*EXEUNT COOKS, Laughing*

**BISHOP:** Let's withdraw. These great conundrums
Fit me not.

**COUNT:** And yet, one size fits all![126]
Come! Come! Hast lost thy appetite for prophesy?
I'll gaze upon this Devils' barbeque.[127]
I'll gnaw the bones and let them read the runes.
Speak, ye Malaprops and Mystic Hams![128]

*To Them, the Weird Cooks and doodlesack*

**1ST COOK:** Four months hath King Bernardo laid a stiff,
And yet no body sits propp'd up
Upon his throne.[129]

---

[125] An antique reference to the Peace of Hebraicus in 1369. Clerical powers were considerably reduced by penile circumcision and the Orders of Disuse as set down by Pope Porus XVXVIII.

[126] Conundrums were to be worn only during the Summer months in Pflegm.

[127] Originally, a dinner held on the Eve of All Souls' Day, now frequently used to describe Republican or law-enforcement get-togethers. Chef Crockette, *as ibid as ever*, concocts a feast including razor-back hog stuffed with razor clams, cuttlefish and whelps, with a sauce hot enough "to make the arse-hole giddy with excitement," as the Chef notes.

[128] "Mystic Hams" is a reference to a loosely formed and secret society of thespians who met after performances to ridicule and parody "the sacred theatre works" in smoke-filled rooms. It has more to do with drink than food. "Malaprop's" was a Bankseyside ale house where actors gathered to run lines with whomever was available.

[129] A Quarto discovered in the Harvard MBA Library reads:
**2ND COOK:** And yet, no Prince sits vested on his throne.
**3RD COOK:** If there's no Royal Head to mint 'pon coin —
**2ND COOK:** Thou'lt needs must send to Spain and beg a loan!

| | |
|---|---|
| **2ND COOK:** | So grasp the moment and the Prince — <br> And ship the potted heirling off to school! |
| **3RD COOK:** | Let greybeard mount the throne and scepter wield. |
| **ALL:** | Lest Pflegmland's court be ruled by a fool! |

*EXEUNT COOKS Laughing. A Thunder Clapp.*

| | |
|---|---|
| **COUNT:** | Speak they of me? Their metaphores are mix'd <br> And thick as gruel.[130] |
| **BISHOP:** | P'raps, good broth', both pottage[131] <br> And the burp-rights will be thine.[132] |
| **COUNT:** | If that be so, <br> Then dare I move askew of Fate?[133] <br> Were I the smallest wren,[134] I would not fly <br> From foddering my feathered babes. <br> Doth not the ermin'd weasel[135] <br> Nose his own hole first?[136] <br> Did not the legendary pachyderm,[137] <br> That loyal parent, push on and on |

---

[130] A Phlegmish country stew, described as being "dark as mulled wine." Tasty!

[131] Pottage is a sturdier variant of the peasants' daily gruel. It not only sticks to the bones but also to brick and is a common mortar in Phlegmish hovels. Known as "pottages," these rude hovels became known as "cottages" as a result of centuries of toothless mispronunciation. AS

[132] These four lines were translated by Chef Crockette in *The Edible Shakespeare*, Thos. Cooke & Sons, London, Second Edition, 1938, into a menu for a "Typical English Oatmeal Breakfast."

[133] Chance. Kismet.

[134] A medieval bird known for excessive mothering, who kept her brood under strict control until they became soaked with their own oils and died. The breed is no more. The line can be read "my oiled babes."

[135] Weasels are known to purchase ermine coats on credit during the winter months in America, in order to supplement their natural fur.

[136] So claimed the 12th century naturalist Shrewdfael of Cadbury in his *Onanum Gatherum*.

[137] The "pachyderm" of legend.

His onyx eggs to Babylon and back?[138]
Doth not the queenly spider seize
And eat her mate?[139]
Ah, well. I'll Queenless be,
And sweetly wax as Rex.
But hold! They say, to rule I needs must die.
If so, I'll be a spook![140]
And fright Prince Edmund off to cold Norway![141]

EXEUNT *Severally. A Clapp of Thunder.*

MUSICK *playes.*

---

[138] Believed to be a reference to the Adamic Mystery, attributed to St. Gnosis of Klym. In it, an elephant wins an egg-rolling contest. See also Aesop, "The Aleph and the Ant."

[139] A story famously re-told in Di Clamaroni's lusty *Boccaccio*, 1645.

[140] "Blackamoor." By King James' time deemed "politically incorrecte."

[141] Pflegmish noblemen often sent their sons to the Odd Bang Skule in Oslo, known then as now as the "Seat of Learning for the Frozen North." No less a scholar than Erasurmus called Odd Bang "the Royal Thing."

*"He perches there upon the tower's tipply top!"*

# ANYTHYNGE YOU WANT TO
## ACTE TWO, SCENE ONE

*The Ramparts of Castle Pflegm. A cock crows.*

ENTER PETE *of Pike, in Armour.*

PETE: The soldier's life, it ain't so grand,
Bend, boys, bend.[142]
But me feets at least is on dry land,
Bend, boys, bend.
Yare! I'll drink me sack, 'till I'm on me back,
While the ground supports me fall!
But the sailor lad, when 'e's drunk 'n' mad
Will sink like a Tinker's ball![143]

ENTER ANDREW[144] *as the* GHOST OF KING BERNARDO[145]

ANDREW: Oooooooo! Edmund!

PETE: 'Od's balls! 'Tis King Bernardo's Ghost again!
Evacuate into the morning mist, unhappy sheet!

ANDREW: Edmund! Me bonny lad!

---

[142] Pete is here performing the Irish Sewer Dance, which "continues lustily 'til break of dawn." Once popular, this extreme form of clog dancing still clogs the public airwaves during fund-raising "specials."

[143] The last Tinkers Union Ball held in America was in Tacoma, Washington, in 1924, after which the profession disappeared.

[144] Sir Andrew Lunch was a real person, a "disembodied Scottish Lorde" who was so thin that he was often not seen at all unless one walked around him. Queen Elizabeth herself was said to have performed unmentionable Toiletries in his presence, unaware that he was watching. He was beheaded in 1613, although the executioner was never sure. "It might have been a shadowe," he was said to have said.

[145] King Bernard II of Hoch Pflegm, known as "The Frail" (1425-1427)

| PETE: | Come not so close, old Spirit cold, |
| --- | --- |
| | Or I'll shred thy shift with me lancelot bold. |
| ANDREW: | 'Old off a mo'! What be thy name, ye rusty clod? |
| PETE: | Pete of Pike, dead Sire. Pike's Pete. |
| | A simple man. |
| ANDREW: | Then gae thae wimple, stupid wae a-bed.[146] |
| | Tho' we be King Bernardo, yet, |
| | We shall relieve thee of thy watch! |
| PETE: | Me watch? |

*EXIT ANDREW, LAUGHING*

| PETE: | Saint Mickey's hands![147] 'E took me watch! |
| --- | --- |
| | That's no relief to me, so, unreliev'd |
| | I must relieve meself, upon yon mossy |
| | Rampart wall, and write in steaming streams |
| | "Bernardus Rex," and dot the "I" for King. |
| | Had I but water left, and time, |
| | I'd fill a moat 'twixt dreadful Wraith and me![148] |

*ENTER ANDREW, as himself*

| ANDREW: | Boo! |
| --- | --- |
| PETE: | Oh! Oh, I am afraid, and fear! |
| ANDREW: | Put up thy pidd'ling Pike, you fool! |
| | That Shade beneath the windin'-sheet was I, |

---

[146] Andrew here attempts to simulate the late King's Pflegmish drawl.

[147] St. Michael of Sebastopol, who was martyred for his sense of humor.

[148] This delightful, oft-performed scene of rustic hilarity features a standard laugh-getting technique of Elizabethan theatre, known as "pissing off," (that is, off stage), or "pissing into the wings." The Groundlings, yelling "Piss on it!", apparently thought nothing was funnier than having an actor urinate on stage, and one can find clowns doing so in such works as Wm. Shakespheare's 2 Henry IV 1, 2, 1: "Sirrah...what says the doctor to my water?"

|                | And I'm Sir Andrew Lunch,[149] the same as e'er, |
|                | Thy rascally relief and faithful battle-mate. |

PETE: Me bottle-mate ye mean! Yer counterfit
Fair put me pants afloat. It's only right
You fill 'em up again![150]

ANDREW: Fear not, Wet Peter[151]
For thee I've brought honest spirits i' the
Drunkard's sack. Here's breakfast toast enough
For both of us! Come, fill thy winklin', tiny cup.

PETE: 'Od's tonsils! We'll meet the dawn with
Peckers[152] up!

*ENTER upon the battlements, the GHOST[153]*

GHOST: Ooooooooo! Edmund!

ANDREW: What's that?

PETE: Tis ghastly King Bernardo, come at dawn!
See, where he stands upon yon battlements.

ANDREW: He seems to float with no more substance
Than me breath. Slip thee to[154] butt'ry down
And fetch the Prince.[155]

---

149 This character was so popular that a rival team of playwrites (Marston, Chapman and Heffeweisen) capitalized on it with "Lunch In Love" (1610).

150 Pflegmish foot soldiers or "walking turds" were outfitted with moleskin bladder-lined shorts or "turd punts" as they were known in the barracks. Urinating while on duty was dubbed "flooding the punts." It's obvious that Andrew's prank has flooded Pete's punts.

151 A popular English sweet made with treacle and alum.

152 Olde English, "spirits." A double-play on drinking. "Peckers" was a variety of Pfligmish ale so potent as to render its drinkers impotent.

153 In some quartos, spelled "Goat." See note 153.

154 "Thy" in the so-called "Rude Quarto."

155 Formerly known as The Prince, he was at this time in his life merely an unpronounceable symbol. (But a symbol of what?)

| PETE: | I go. We'll meet again, I 'ope! |

*EXIT PETE, afeard.*

| GHOST: | Ooooooooo! |

| ANDREW: | 'Tis surely he!<br>He sports the sacred Hat upon his shroud. |

| GHOST: | Eternal sleep sits moistly 'pon my face<br>These clammy nights.[157] Once more I walk<br>These slipp'ry withering heights,<br>In aimless, mindless searching<br>For a man with blunted aim<br>And motley tights!<br>Edmund! |

*ENTER PRINCE EDMUND, with Pete, Soldiers and SWEET MARIE.*

| ED: | Where be it? Show it me! |

| MARIE: | But, sweet my Lord, I have.[158] |

| ED: | Nay, Sweet Marie. I'm speaking to these soldiers here. |

| PETE: | Mark! It seems to float like oil upon the sea! |

| ED: | I'll be not gull'd! Hand me my sword-flask, man! |

| ANDREW: | What use is sober steel against a Ghost, my Prince? |

---

[156] See Edmund Edmund's speech, Act II, ii.

[157] The Pflegmish were insatiable nocturnal clam fishermen. In the fortnight between Muckle Mouse and the Quincunx of Mars the locals rushed to the shore and clamed all night; thus the term "clamor," signifying the awful brouhaha these mollusk munchers made.

[158] Gender confusion, cross-dressing and female role-playing make their first appearance in *AYWT* along with Sweet Marie. She is absent from the earliest printings of the play, and is thought to have been added by Wm. Shakespeare in his aforementioned re-write, probably for his "close friend" the transexual actor Little Jim.

| | |
|---|---|
| **MARIE:** | A Ghost? |
| **PETE:** | It hops up King Bernardo's crumbling tower, m'lord. |
| **ED:** | The goats? |
| **MARIE:** | The Ghost, sweet Prince. |
| **ED:** | Methought they spoke of goats[159] upon the battlements! |
| **PETE:** | Nay, Ghost, m'lord. |
| **ED:** | Well, be he Ghost, or goat, or ghost of goat Or both, I'll spirits need to goad my spirits on![160] |
| **GHOST:** | Edmund! |
| **ANDREW:** | See! The spook would speak with thee! |
| **MARIE:** | He perches there, upon the tower's tipply top![161] |
| **ED:** | I'm here, deceased Parent. |
| **GHOST:** | Thou poor, unfocus'd Prince. Get thee anon to Norway! |
| **ED:** | Back to school? I learn'd there all I could and burn'd it down![162] I doubt they'll have me back! |

---

[159] The goats of Mont Pflegm are still occasionally to be seen, although they are reportedly slightly radioactive.

[160] The spirits referred to here is the fermented rancid goat milk that for centuries has winnowed out the Pflegmish lower classes. It's not the fouled goat's milk that gives the drink its fatal punch, but the toxic thimbleweed extract that is added to mask the drink's nauseating back-taste.

[161] The tipply top was a common feature of late medieval Pflegmish castle architecture. It was a tower nook, easily concealing the late night reveler or goldbricking turd who choose to empty their flasks and punts unseen.

[162] The Odd Bang Skule (a School of Drama) in Oslo (then Christiana), was burned to the ground during a student revolt in 1597, as Shakespeare well knew.

GHOST: To Norway go!
Where nights like day are followed fast by days
Of endless night, and buxom Viking dames
Quaff aquavit![163]

MARIE: Go not, sweet virgin Prince. This, thy Father's
'Fernal shade, leads thee up to Hell!

GHOST: Ooooooooo!

ED: If that be Hell, I'll to't, and snort at fate!
What's Hell to me, or me to Hell?
What th'Hell?[164]
As a tiny tot my Mother told me not to cross
The moat, but then the Monk, he did bespeak me,
Cast the moat from thine own eye!
And so confus'd, I cross'd mine eyes and
Double-cross'd the Monk, who fell into the moat!
Then thou, my nice and naughty niece, Marie,
Did give me warning I play no longer with myself,
'Twould make me blind! I was not deaf to thy
Entreaties, and so I lept into her burning bush,
And lo, altho' consum'd by fire, I rose again
To bite another apple on yet another Eve!
Afraid of Hell?
I've left my senses many times, and dream'd
I fought great monsters, pachyderms of pink,
In pond'rous packs, like rats upon my bed.

---

[163] From *aqua vitae*, "water of life." A sort of liquid bread served frozen in a block of ice. See Chef Croquette, *ibid*.

[164] The beginning of this version of Edmund's famous soliloquy is based a late 18th century revision of the text. The earliest MSS have:

ED: 'ell! 'ell? What's 'ell? They tore it down!
What's 'ell to me or me to 'ell? What th'ell?

The learned reference to "tearing down the 'ell" was lost on later audiences. This great speech was "translated" in Donald B. Lindley's "An Analysis of The Schizophrenic Thought and Language of The Firesign Theatre" (Lone Mountain College, 1973, unpublished):

"When I was a child, my parents demanded of me strict adherence to certain forms of behavior. They told me that I'd go to Hell if I disobeyed. They told me not to masturbate, but I ignored their command and did it anyway, and I felt guilty about it. I then discovered sex with women, blamed the women for seducing me, and felt guilty about it. I turned to alcohol as a relief from my guilt. I even have hallucinations and bad dreams that monsters will punish me for my transgressions, although I try to give the appearance

|  | Who cares?[165] Are we not men? |
|---|---|
| **MARIE:** | Not I, my Lord. |
| **ED:** | If we fall down, can not we rise again?[166]<br>Hot-headed, flushed with blood,<br>We'll not take it lying down! We'll stand it up!<br>And get it any way we can![167]<br>St. Mickey,[168] save me! |
| **GHOST:** | Shut up, Edmund! |
| **EDMUND:** | You see? He knows me!<br>For Grid,[169] for Goofy and St. Walt![170]<br>Have at you! |

---

that I don't believe in Hell, that I am guilt-free, and unafraid of retribution. I want an inordinate amout of sex to prove to my parents that I'm my own boss. I need some magic to save me from my driven, guilt-ridden existence."

[165] The Hubble Collection ms continues:
    ED:      I've been in service of the Martial Mars and viewed blue skies
                Turned rusty by the redden'd dust. Seen good green Earth
                All yellow-soaked with fear. Blood-covered, blistered,
                black-pocked like Luna's back.

[166] Later used by Sir Edmund Fudde as the second of five "Rules of Principles of Gravitie Explaynd." Fudde extracted the first, "*Intrat et exit ut nil supra*," from Vini ille Pooh by Milnus the Elder.

[167] The "Kartoom Illuminated MS" has this sentiment added:
    ED:      Saint Mickey save me!
       I'll wiggle my ears and march forth full of song
       And give my finger to the first who follows not.

[168] In the Great Folio of 1699, "St. Viagra, save me!" St. Mickey lost his ears in the War of Mickey's Ear (1687). St. Viagra is patron saint of stand-up comedians. St. Condom, sometimes inserted, was banished from the Irish Church along with snakes.

[169] Mark B. Aickelin's exhaustive 2005 work, *The Simple English Schoolboy's Decoding Manual*, points out that a grid is a part of an improved vacuum tube which envelops the cathode filament thus attracting and accelerating electrons flowing from it. The name "grid" was coined by *the electrician* (emphasis ED) Lee de Forest in 1906. The "Audion" tube (see "The Zeppelin Tube" of Hemlock Stones fame, ED) is thus an *amplifier* and led directly to the invention of radio. "Empire of the Air," a radio epic by David Ossman, dramatizes this story, which, interesting as it is, has nothing to do with Saint Grid. See below.

[170] Often called the Pflegmish Trinity, Sts. Grid, Goophous and Walto (or "Waldo") were three brothers first frozen for their espousal of the Deconstructive Heresy, then warmed in a slow oven. Chef Crockette's Easter Trefoil Cakes are made the same way, stuffed with a local sausage known as Blootwurst.

**MARIE:** See how his Pflegm doth rise!

*The GHOST approacheth.*

**GHOST:** To Norway, Edmund!

**ED:** Aye, dear, dead Dad!
I'll abdicate the Crown,
My coronation skip[171] and leave at once
To be your Midnight Son. But first,
Let me embrace thee!

**GHOST:** Nay! Stay back!

**ED:** I'll clamber up to claim thy clammy draperies![172]

**GHOST:** 'Twill ruin all!

**ED:** I'll race to ruin!
I'll bite thy wan and waxen lips,
And draw refreshing nectar
From thy hollow kiss.

**GHOST:** Nay, stay! Dawn comes!
I needs must slip away!

**PETE:** And so he does.

**MARIE:** And slipping, shows his knees, revealing
Blue and goosley flesh!

---

[171] Another Fyre Sygne pun. The Coronation Skip was a festive line dance that celebrated the crowning of a sovereign and rubbed royal salt in the wounds of the pretenders who had been skipped over. In its ancient form, the dance was more a gauntlet than a minuet. Those in line for the throne who had been cheated of their birthright were made to skip down a double row of the new monarch's heftiest favorites. These louts would pummel the pretender with oaken "skip sticks" until they were thoroughly dead and no longer a threat to anyone. The word skeptic evolved from this ritual, denoting one who had grave doubts about contesting the succession to the throne. AS

[172] A reference to the Pflegmish loose-fitting "clamming clothes" they sported during the brief bivalve harvest. [See footnote 152 *et. seq.*] Lithographs of these outfits were prominent in the works of Andreaus Whirrwhole and soon sparked a continent-wide fashion fad. The "clammer look" became synonymous with enticing beauty and comes down to us today as "glamour." AS

**ED:** Stay, royal parent!][173]

*EDMUND follows after the GHOST.*

**ANDREW:** Edmund reaches out, yet touches naught but air.[174]

**GHOST:** Get back! Back off! Aaagh . . .

*EXIT the GHOST, falling*

**ED:** He's gone.

**ANDREW:** 'Tis dawn.

**PETE:** 'Tis done.

**ED:** 'Tis well 'tis dawn. 'Tis done.

**MARIE:** He's gone.

**ANDREW:** He's fallen to the sea![175]

**MARIE:** Follow not, Prince Edmund, lest a ghost ye be.

**ED:** King Bernardo walks again, and bids me leave! What does this mean? Come men!

**MARIE:** Not I, my Lord.

**ED:** And you, Marie.
Bring on the nuts and ales and meat.
We'll speak of this anon.

---

[173] The lines between brackets are missing from the Great Folio. The Ghost merely says "Back off!" and vanishes off stage.

[174] Rick Shakespeare added this line in 1980 for the Pflegmish Radio production "on the psychic advice of my ancestor, Wm., who demanded narration for sightless viewers."

[175] A line attributed to the great clown "Spike" Mulligan, uttered in the 1980 broadcast.

MARIE: And on and on and on!

ED: But first, let's eat![176]

*EXEUNT OMNES. A Musickal Interlude.*

---

[176] A charming Elizabethan sentiment and food for thought.

*"For Grid, for Goofy and St. Walt!"*
*Wiggan Cuppe as Edmund*
*Shakespeare in the Dark (1973)*

# ANYTHYNGE YOU WANT TO
## Acte Two, Scene Two

*The Sea-Shore, near Castle Pflegm.*

ENTER FLOUNDER, a Beachcomber[177] and his Children.

FLOUNDER[S]: 1[Come childeren, my pretty little frys.[178]
You, Hake and Shad, your brothers help to draw
The weighty Oyster nets, and silent be,
For noise annoys each love-cross'd double-valve,
Or Mollusk in his briny, simp'ring doze.]
2[Go Winkle, and fair Cockle, help thy Mum,
The lab'ring Queen of this our fishy fief,
To cure the crabs and ground the glowing Eel.]
3[Limpet, hang cod-piece and perch-pelt side-beside,
That they may dry from last night's stormy pour.
I will walk here, a Monarch on this pearly strand,
And comb for bounty of the 'zausted Hurricane.]
2[As I be despot o'er this useless bay,
I'll tax the sea that spends all night upon
The shore.] 3[I'll tythe the tide, and take percentage
Of the typhoon's toll. A trunk of Ruby-wood,
Wind-ripp'd from far-off Philipine, mayhaps,]
1[Or graceful Amphorae, fill'd full of Ancient Grease,]

---

[177] The Beachcombers of Pflegmland's "Cote d'Ebris" — a strand on the Bay of Iceland where marine flotsom from as far away as India still collects among the WWII mine fields and U-Boat bunkers — were renowned in Northern European folklore. They often combed in groups of three, which, if so staged, would alter the distribution of the dialog as noted.

[178] Flounder's speech is a virtual menu of seafare of the times. The legendary Fisher of Elizabethan beaches was a figure known to frighten children. Here, he is seen as a beneficent father, whose children are as well-nigh edible as the creatures cured and ground by Mumm, his legendary wife. (In Ireland, Mumm is an evil witch who rides in a helicopter to barracks in Northern Ireland and quickly vanishes. In France, she is a bacchanalian Queen of Grape. In America, she's the word. And, don't you know, the Word is Love.)

2[Or even find a rich-tool'd wallet, gilt anchor[179]
Of some drown'd and bloated Turk.[180]]
3[What's this?
A heap of ebon'd kelp?]

*Enter EDMUND EDMUND, asleep upon the sand.*

ED ED: Oh! Oh!

FLOUNDER: 3[It lives!]
1[Art Ethiope, or tarry Babe from storied Remus'[181]
Briar-patch'd shores?]

ED ED: What, fool! Old foul-smelling fish!
Did I survive the Winter Tempest's Tale[182]
To be bombarded by this bouillebaisic bard?[183]
Give aid! I am thy rightful King!

FLOUNDER: 2[Nay, pitchy Jonah. I be fisher-king,
While thou'rt nothing but a king of fish,]
3[Unlike the unicorn'd Narwhal, who keeps

---

[179] The "guilt anchor" is a loose reference to Aquinas' monumental treatise *Vacuus Opulentia Illic Est Haud Sin*. ("Without Wealth There Is No Sin"). This 13th century intellectual giant was as poor as he was prolific, subsisting for decades on little else than groat cakes and cistern scrapings. His self-inflicted penury radically affected his attitude toward the merest accumulation of worldly goods. In the Saint's own words: *Tantum perficio penuriosus can ingredior per Sarcalogos super aequora. Haud is anchor extraho suum animus ut Abyssus*. ("Only the perfected poor can walk with Christ upon the waters. No golden anchor drags their souls to hell.")

[180] Turkish seamen traded with Pflegmish burghers as early as the 17th century, exchanging hashish for gin and semen for burgers.

[181] Another indication that the Author or Authors ventured to the New World. Remus (*R'ximm'iis*) is an Osage Indian figure from the Myth of Origin who "frighted the Rabbits from this world." He should not be confused with "Rebus" Caneebis, an historical figure of much later date, said mistake giving the lie to much of Goncourt's suppositions. "Rebus" is found in the "P. C. Quarto."

[182] This reference is the primary justification for E. R. Bothelin's assignment of the authorship of this play to Wm. Shakesp[h]eare and not, as had been previously assumed, to Richard Greene, that "Tyger's Heade wrapt in poore Shatsphere's hearte" who claimed until his death in 1634 that it was he who wrote it. He, too, seemed unsure of the title.

[183] One of the finest lines of poetry in this, or any other, Elizabethan play. The American tragedian Edwin Garrett was said to have relished the playing of it so that he once had to be physically stopped from repeating the sentence over and over again at a performance in New York, " . . . until the gas ran out of the lamps and the audience stood enraged." (See Shenannigan's *Final Curtains I Have Known*, privately published, Boston, 1901.)

>    His oil within his bladder trapp'd,[184] thy oil
>    Is all without, upon thy face and limbs.]

**ED ED:** Back off, Buffoon! I'll wipe myself
And, stagg'ring, stand up while I do't.
This oil I wear is mine, and mine alone!
I'd carried back from New Verginie's
Tideland pools four thousand barrels worth.
Now all, all lost! The New World's pow'r
Sunk useless to the bottom of the sea!

**FLOUNDER:** 1[[Nay, 'tis not. Christlike, it rises as ye speak!]
2[Upon me soul, 'tis 'pon the bottom of me boot!]
3[By St. Exxon's broken hull[185]! It's here! It's there!]
omnes[It's all o'er everywhere!]

**ED ED:** Good news is this, old [you] flat-fac'd, one-eyed man [men] [dame]!
We'll strain it from the sand, and thus refin'd,
Find purpose in its several qualities.
Go, blowfish, go! Run up to Castle Pflegm
And puff this message in the Bishop's privy ear:
"Double E hath from the C emerg'd
And R would B."[186]

**FLOUNDER:** 1[Slip me but a fin, and swift I'll pass it on.]

**ED ED:** Then, Shark, take thou this golden Crown
From out my Jaws. But show it to my Nuncle first.
I faint.

**FLOUNDER:** 2[He faints. I'll leave him where he lays.]
3[High tide will wash him back to old Poseidon's grave.]

*EXIT Flounder*

---

184 An observation made by Aristotle, but biologically unsound. Narwal oil is kept in the liver, and once was both a popular lubricant and English sweet.

185 St. Exxon of Aleutia is patron saint of strip-miners and oil-well-fire-extinguishers. He was broken on the wheel in 1347 during the Fourth Crusade.

186 A puzzle in the style of the Roman poet known as "Uncle Rebus," c. 37 AD.

**ED ED:** All oiled thus, I'll slip up on his [her] tasty Wife
While he's away. A shipwreck'd Rex twixt
Heaving bosoms, safe as sushi[187] shall I lay!

*A Doleful INTERLUDE*[188]

---

[187] Evidently another reference to the Asian pirate ship which allegedly brought Edmund Edmund back to Pflegm. Unhappily the entire crew must have lost their lives in the always bitter and tempestuous Finland Straits.

[188] Note that the later Fyre Sgne Thtre, seeking, perhaps, more speeches for its players, routinely performed this scene by dividing Flounder's lines up for three actors — Flounder and his two sons "Roister" and "Oyster."

*"Cares who for ratones, mi Lord? Pas yo."*
*Antonia Chortears as Maria la Fea in "Cualquiero que tu quieres" at Teatro del Barrio & Grill, 2002*

# ANYTHYNGE YOU WANT TO
## ACTE TWO, SCENE THREE

*The Tower. The Bishop's Cell.*

*BUBBLING of retorts. DRIPS. Of Mice, their SQUEEKS. Of owls, their HOOTS.*

*ENTER The BISHOP, together with SWEET MARIE.*

**BISHOP:** See how my hot retort doth bubble up?[189]
Now thy retort I'll hear, sweet virgin maid.

**MARIE:** Again, my Lord Archbishop?
This stuffy tower with its 'noxious Fumes
Splits the tiny Atoms of my throbbing Brain.
What's Alchemie to me, or me to Alchemie?[190]
Must I repeat that Formula anon?
It drives me daft!

**BISHOP:** Absolutely, Sweet Marie! 'Tis wizzard's fun.[191]
'Twill make thee wise as I.
Say: "Four times revolve the rodent round

---

[189] The Bishop fits the standard model of the time for a phlegmatic, or hot, personality. "Bubble Up" was a common alchemical drink mentioned by Regiomantus in the *Profecies of Gruber* (1567.)

[190] This extraordinary reversible incantation was to the Medieval Black Arts what "abracadabra" was to the Pyramid scheming Arabs of 14th century Fez. The Bishop invokes the immense complimentarity of matter and spirit to "walk that narrow Planck Space 'tween the two and 'nipulate the motes of dust that mold the world." See Olaf Bonefolder's spinning doctorate, *We're All Bosons On This Quark*, Annals of Post Particle Physics, June 1973.

[191] "Wizard's fun" refers to the secret art of fellatio perfected by the cohort of "Tickled Frenchmen," a reckless order of hedonists that lists among its members, (*sic*) Aristophanes, Casanova, Benjamin Franklin, Ramon Navarro and George Clooney. Two lines hence, the Bishop refers to the chief device of this amorous

In Friar Swiggen's spit."[192]
Come! Come!
"Then Salt of chaste St. Peter take,
And dip it in his . . ."[193]

**MARIE:** No! No! How it dulls me,
This turning little mice to lead.

**BISHOP:** And thence, with thy as yet unspoil'd assistance,
Into little mice of gold.[194]

**MARIE:** Cares who for mice, my Lord? Not I.
I'd wear a Fool's gold and be a Queen,
And Queens have need of other chemistry.

**BISHOP:** React not so rapidly, Marie!

**MARIE:** He does not court me, nor rule my court,
This playful Edmund.
He who served me but one time,
Now serves me not at all,
But bounces out-of-bounds, to Norway,
Other scores to seek.

**BISHOP:** What's love but nothing? Play a better game.
Your Jack's a knave, forget his suit,
Another Joker lies within your pack tonight.[195]

---

diversion as "the revolving rodent in Friar Swiggen's spit." Swiffen, a notorious 13th century Troubadour, penned this famous quatrain:
> Recline Oh, aching goddess
> And let my tongue proclaim
> The joys that lie thy chamber in
> That thee might come again. [AS]

**192** "Fr. Swiggin's Spitte" was a broadsword upon which heretics and non-Conforming Cattle were slowly barbequed. The results, we are told, in *The Good Hus-wifes Jewell*, were delicious.

**193** Here, the Author or Authors are having the audience "on." The Formula, "Philtre d'Amour" is derived from the *Booke Of Cerebral Magicks* (early 14th century), and concludes "*Matrice d'une hirondelle, un rognon de lievre/Poudre sal de S. Pierre, et de lui meme le merdre.*"

**194** Lead mice were considered charms for good fishing. Gold mice, though never seen, were considered alchemically feasible by most practitioners of the time. Their use would have been in creating cartoons, we suppose.

**195** Professor Rumble Skillsin opines, in his *Closet Whist And Other Ludic Heresies* (Charnel House, Blackberry,

**MARIE:** Are we at whist, my Lord?

**BISHOP:** Call it "Diplomacy."[196]
'Tis very like the sport of cards, my dear.
We deal to win. Soon thou must bid thy hand.

**MARIE:** I'll bid! A deuce of hearts!

**BISHOP:** Ah, Douche![197] 'Tis better you should bid
Adieu[198] to abdicating Edmund.

**MARIE:** Nay, reverend Father.
If I'm to keep possession, then I must make
Good sport with him, in Nature's oldest Game.

**BISHOP:** That's out! Come back to Books and Physick.

**MARIE:** My heart is melted down. I'm fusing at the core!
If Edmund thinks he's led me on,
I'll let his heat transform my leaden Mouse
To Golden Ore.[199]

*MARIE EXITS at a run. The BISHOP, alone.*

**BISHOP:** Really! My experiments in magnifying pow'r
Do threat to run awry.
And so, these diverse elements
Needs I must rectify.
First, sweet ward Marie —

---

1968) that "the Joker" is in fact "Satan's poker" [or "porker" Ed.] that "flushed out many a full house of royal Queens," an obvious allusion to the frosty court of Prestone I, the anti-Frisian pontiff.

[196] An Elizabethan game similar to chess.

[197] A cleansing of the hand after sneezing (Low Middle Pflemish).

[198] *A-dieu*, a late-Frankish variant of "Ah, Douche." (See previous footnote.) Said after shaking hands good-bye.

[199] The Derrick Escrow production of *AYWT* for Raadio Pflegm used a version of this text altered by the 19th century English prelate and anti-smut crusader, the Ultra Rt. Rev. Thurmond Helms, O. D. It suppresses Marie's potential "over reaction," and leaves the Power in the hands of the Bishop. Escrow claimed he merely "needed to get on with it."

> She's Elmo's running fire[200] uncontain'd,
> And should she touch quicksilver Edmund,
> His Mercury will doubtless rise.[201]
> Better she should warm pig-headed Edmund
> Edmund's iron will, and turn him thus red-hot!
> Alloy'd so, he'll steal the precious Crown — for me!

ENTER FLOUNDER, ATTENDED BY TWO MONKES[202]

**FLOUNDER (ASIDE):** Now, here's the Devil-Fishe at work I see,
And so I'll fish up from the deeps of memory
The baited hook.
(ALOUD) Sire! List to me! "Double E hath —
from the C emerg'd and R would B!"

EXIT FLOUNDER, chaste as a Monke.[203]

**BISHOP:** The shrimp bespeaks an alphabet of welcome news.
As Edmund Edmund comes, so goes the Count.
My sulph'rous cooks[204]
Did tarnish well his silver-halo'd head
With thoughts of Kingdoms come, and yet,
So backwardly he feign'd the ghostly King Bernard
That he fell backward to the sea
And nearly drown'd.
So lastly I myself.
My mettle heavier than all of these,

---

[200] St. Elmo, martyred by burning, has been adopted in our time as patron saint of telephone solicitors.

[201] An astrological reference. If Edmund's "rising sign" was Mercury, he was, we are told by no less an authority than Sir Robert Fudde, in his *Utriusque Cosmi Historica* (1619), "apte to expend his Manhoode recklesslie."

[202] His lines, and those of the Bishop following are a crude narrative device to bring the audience up-to-speed if they had missed anything in the general noise, bustle and confusion of Shakesphere's theatre.

[203] An abbreviation of "Monkefish," the only member of its genus that after initial procreation turns to abuse the younger members of its school.

[204] Salt was not introduced into the Pflegmish kitchen until it was imported from Bulgaria during The Endless War of Reform for rubbing in the wounds of Protestant prisoners. It soon replaced sulfur as the primary condiment, vastly improving the breath and pallor of the country's gourmands.

>Of undiscovered substances contrived.[205]

*FLOUNDER ENTERS once againe*
>Am I then doom'd to live but half-a-life
>Upon this narrow Island, but three miles wide,[206]
>While my ambition's melted down to smoking slag?
>Nay!
>Within the bubbling pot, confusion is the key.
>To make full newly clear the Pow'r
>Must my Reaction be![207]

*FLOUNDER DIVES INTO THE POT*[208]

*A CLOUD OF HEMPISH SMOKE*[209]

*MUSICK of a Doleful Interlude.*[210]

---

[205] Flounder (first played by the great Elizabethan clown Burt Lyon) has here a brief "for a bow" return to the stage, which involved playing broadly to the house and continuing to cut up during the Bishop's reprise of the plot. It was cut from the Escrow radio production "for reasons of time."

[206] Visigoth legend speaks of a Rouber Oppen-Heimer (low Goth for "world destructor") who appeared to their ancestors "in za clod of mushroom schmokes nur Trident Isle, mit fusioned sun von one hant und verld's end zin ozer."

[207] Here, in the Elizabethan theatre, there was "suc a clagging of drummes and symbols as to eraise the ded," according to our old friend Jan Groot.

[208] Burt Lyon's closing stunt was "as a fissshe mite dive upon the see." (Groote, op.cit.)

[209] This scene clearly entranced the unsophisticated Groote who "ston'd as a clam didst misremember where I wast."

[210] During this "doleful interlude," according to Groote, "ho's didst lingere, and appelgirls, shewin of ther wares, of which I nacht partook, feardst o the pox."

*"Excuse, but do we dress to right or left?"*
*Wiggan Cuppe as Pierre de Cardentte*
*in Touch-Your-Tit Theatre's 2005 mime version*

# ANYTHYNGE YOU WANT TO
## Acte Three, Scene One

*The Closet of the COUNT. He ENTERS with Courtiers in attendance.*

*A Consort of Musick playes.*

**COUNT:** If clothing be the skin of Kings,[211]
Dress on, Cardentte!
Give me excess of them, dear Chevrolet!

**CAR:** Oui, oui, mon Seigneur.

**COUNT:** We must be over-hung with silks, that habil'd so,
No peasant rebel's fork[212] in revolution rais'd,
Shall touch our naked self. I dearly love
These furried robes, Pierre.

**CAR:** 'Tis a basse deal[213] at twice the cost, no lese,
Majeste.

---

209 A paraphrase of Innes Voge's "*Peau de Roi:*"
   I'll Coach thee Bebe Zegna,
   And Givanchy the Secret of Victoria's Gap
   That 'pon the Yves of St. Laurent
   Doth Dolce step in Blanik's boots
   To cat-like walk the Prada of Versace town
   With wafer-thin Patek Phillipe
   And crying "Gucci up!"
   Oblivious of Lacoste
   Bags Hermes, Jimmies Chu, doth Hugo Boss,
   To Rolex all within her Cartier of gold.

212 A reference commonly used to date the play's authorship to later than 1599, the year of the Pflegmish Peasant's Rebellion in which the Peasants refused to eat with forks.

213 Bass were twice as expensive as Cod in the London Fishwiferie.

COUNT: Call us not King of Pflegm until his astral Majesty
The Sun shall rise with us tomorrow morn
And crown us one with him.[214]
Hold the mirror so, good Fangboner!

FANG: I will, without reflection, Liege.[215]

*ENTER PESTIO, a Clown.*

PESTIO: Hey, nonny Nuncle! Is it not true
As Pope doth poop in woods,[216] that Sun King's reign
Can clouded and eclipsed be by hidden sons?

COUNT: Nay, Fool! And Fool thou art! 'Tis known[217] that
Bears and Moons do eat the Sun.

PESTIO: I speak of Midnight Sons.

COUNT: That Son has set his sails for Norseland
On the coming Tide.

---

[214] Certainly a jibe, perhaps a cautionary one, directed at the pretentions of King Enery The 'Ateth, for whom his French *cuisinieur* Yves St. Stool (1555?-1603), created Stuffed Codpiece in the Tudor Manner. Chef Crocket, *Ibid.* as ever, stuffs the Cod with Gooey Ducks.

[215] William, Earl of Fangboner (1498-1600) was disguised in the earliest printings of *AYWT* simply as "Extra." Nineteenth century productions usually cut the part — a servile Tudor toady who gave the practice of "fangbonering" its infamous name — at the insistence of the servile Tory todies who acted as theatrical censors. See Sam Shopphard's 1988 comedy, *Fangboner Is Too*.

[216] Here, Shakesphere may be drawing from Chaucer's "The Pope's Nose Tale." Bruno the Bishop of Berzerkfurt was the bastard son of a Silesian poacher who traded the boy to a local monastery for an assortment of indulgences, a knuckle bone of St. Osthman and a demijohn of Chartreuse. Bruno remained an avid hunter before and after his ascension to the papacy as Innocent The Last. During the annual hunt for heretics Bruno was separated from the party and became lost in the Calabrian woods. He was discovered later defecating on the carcass of an enormous bear whose skin he was wearing to ward off whatever chill his flagon of Chartreuse had failed to abate. Thus sprung the rhetorical epithet, "Doth the Pope Not Shite On The Bear in the Woodes?" The saying was later toned down for for use as a cautionary for little children. The more decorous "poop" replaced "shite" and the bear disappeared altogether.

[217] It is thought that Pflegmland's prehistoric inhabitants carved talismans of narwal teeth in the shape of a bear grasping a solar disk in a futile attempt to ward off an anticipated solar eclipse. (See *Annals of the Pflegmish Pfolkloric Psociety*, U. Oxx. CD-ROM Set APPP 1928 HSBN 35196-01010P.) Pflegm itself was the scene of a 1927 total eclipse of the sun. The country lay completely within the path of totality, observed by the crowned heads of Europe in the company of the Pflegmish Astronomer Royal Colslav N. Patatasalat.

**PESTIO:** And like the Tide, young Edmund ebbs and flows!

**FANG:** This flapping, fustion'd Fool ill suits thee, Liege.

**CAR:** Unlike thy Coronation gown!
It slips on like a thin French Glove.
Excuse, but dress we to the left or right?

**PESTIO:** Why, Froggy, he knows not, for lackeys dress him;
And he hath no lack of them, eh, Fangboner?

**COUNT:** Pestio, be still! Loyal Fangboner, you are my
First in Court. Thou soon wilt Chamberlain be,
And, standing tall, will stretch to dunk
The Holy Hoop[218] upon our Kingly Dome.

**FANG:** My lord, I hope it will rebound well for me.

**PESTIO:** Coach him not! He'll dribble out rewards to all!

**FANG:** I fear no foul, Fool. I know I'll get my shot!

*The COURT doth present an Exhibition of Ringe Balle.*[219]

**CAR:** Pardon, mon Liege,
But should the stoats not Rampant be?[220]
These Civet cats lie down upon the sleeves?[221]

**COUNT:** Oh, how the full Court presses me!
'Twill be my sudden death![222]

---

[218] This is a better interpretation of a word that starts with "h," rather than the "hat" of Act 1, sc. 1. A hoop was a word of Old French derivation which originally meant "peach basket." Hat is just a stupid word.

[219] A profound expertise in this game was required of all Pflegmish courtiers. The skill required to catch a small wooden ball between the exposed buttocks and then hurl it accurately through a two-foot hoop, is considerable.

[220] The armorial bearings of the Pflegmish Royal House were, "or, on a bend sable, three stoats rampant, au natural." This was also, according to the redoubtable Chef Crockett, of *ibid* fame, a popular national dish.

[221] Another of the wretched excesses of Ennery the 'Ateth and his court, where civet *parfum* went through a brief vogue during the Black Plague epidemic, doubtless to cover "*le scent du cimitiere.*" (See Old French, *les fents funebres.* Civet pelts were used as oramentation only by the noble classes.

[222] For a complete textual analysis of this exchange, see Alan Bennett's astonishing *Sports Analogies in Shakespeare and Philip Marlowe*, Random Access House, Lerndon Towne, 1989.

*The COUNT retires, with his retinue.*

FANG: 'Tis all set down upon the Scroll of Arms
That's stuff'd within the Sacred Hat.[223]
Go fetch the Bishop, Pestio, and bid him pull
The ancient Parchment out.

PESTIO: Thus to see the ordure of his 'scent to pow'r.

FANG: What, fool?

PESTIO: I'd see to't, Sir, but him you send me seek
I seem to see! And 'side him someone unforseen!
And yet I speak so fast, I know not what I mean!

*PESTIO EXITS, frightened. FANGBONER WITHDRAWS behind a tapestry.*

*ENTER EDMUND EDMUND with THE BISHOP, furtively.*

*A DUMB SHOW.*[224] *FANGBONER IS SLAIN.*

*THEY EXIT.*

---

[223] Or "hoop"? Possibly "pot" or "lid." "Key" has been suggested by Pflegmish historian A. Peteratzy, noting the golden keys on the one-time Royal Family crest. PG

[224] Purely a matter of taste. Many find the Show profoundly diverting. AS

*"Ah, humorous. I thought ye looked for Truth!"*
*Buster Artunian as "Mole"*
*Grip-Your-Bone Playhouse, Provincetown, 2001*

# ANYTHYNGE YOU WANT TO
## ACTE THREE, SCENE TWO

*A GATED CHURCHYARD within the Precincts of Castle Pflegm. GRAVES, one op'd. The SONGS of Birds.*

*MOLE,[225] a gravedigger, digges. ENTER HOLE, a Rustick Clown.*

**HOLE:** Greetings, gates! 'Tis Hole!
And open, gates, so's I might shovel forth
Into yon churchyard low, where labors Brother Mole
Upon some dusty dig. Hole I be, once jester to a pirate king,
But here marooned 'pon Pflegmland's foggy shore
It seems two thousand year. But, labor being labor, here
Hole and Mole most gravely work upon the ends
Poor humans reach, when they're sent home to dust
By hands unknown.
Brief lives, they flower forth through several stages,
Like unto a Chinese rocket smuggled forth:
The first burst but a smiling loaf of doughy genes,
Pacified and left betide where bonny beanie babies sing.
Then, all too soon, a blotch-faced schoolboy, soccer-shoe'd,
Who pass them must, th' gruesome tests
His fathers never met. Then suddenly as Spring,
The simple-minded lover, airy-stringed guitar at hand,
A ballad belting forth
Upon his busty babe's be-ringed brow.
Next, in self-concern'd oblivion, his body couched potato-like

---

[225] Both of these characters were at one time essayed by each of the greatest of the Elizabethan clowns, Rob't Armin and Louie Louis. Each made his greatest reputation in the role, but there was much confusion at the time as to who was whom and, for that matter, which role was which. In later years, the Great Shinannigan himself, teamed with John Drew Booth, would often play both parts until Booth knocked him into the "grave" with his shovel. Of course, modern Funny Man Teams like Ford & Chevy and Cheech & Chase, and even the Austman Brothers have vied for the opportunity to pair up in this scene.

> Upon the beer-stain'd frat-room floor, he plays a tiny game
> Of deadly strife and thus exhausts his dextrous thumbs.
> At last, a man of parts,
> Suited in the narrow-collar'd Roman style,
> Stretch-limo'd, meetings ta'en, buying, selling,
> Hearty reputation all a-bubble 'neath his silken tie.
> And when the stress-built bubble bursts,
> He droppeth down as doth a stone,
> And ever shall he sleep right here,
> Within his holy wooden scull, one full-moon'd tide above
> The storm. And in that brewing storm
> Shall all his mortal dust be launch'd
> Without a moment's bruhaha upon the deep blue sea.[226]

*MOLE stands forth from the grave.*

**HOLE:** Yare down there, Mole! Riddle me this one!

**MOLE:** Wait, Hole! I cannot dig and think together.
I'll stop. I'm stopping. I've stopped.

**HOLE:** Why is yer common gravedigger like unto yer coarse common actor?

**MOLE:** Oh. 'Cause we're in the same Guild.[227]

**HOLE:** Yer right. We share the same Guild, that's true.
But that's not the funny answer, maggot-pate![228]

*MOLE turns up a bone. He lookes at it.*

**MOLE:** Ah, humorous. I thought ye looked for Truth.

---

[226] Hole's speech was edited from the Raadio Pflegm broadcast. Escrow called it "spurious!" It is, however a frequent audition piece in regional theatre.

[227] The Congress of Grave Makers and Coarse Actors, founded in 1302. Also, by its members, known as Ye Smoked Hammes. This guild had, since the 14th century, presented the Pageant of Unlucky Job at Christmastide in Thamesbottom.

[228] The Maggot Pate was a popular hairstyle among the lowest classes in Elizabethan England. A bowl of starved maggots was placed on the client's head and removed after the hungry larvae had had their fill, revealing a close-cropped "cruel cutte." The method delivered an added bonus as the maggots ate hair and lice alike.

| | |
|---|---|
| **HOLE:** | Yer horeson gravemaker is like unto yer playactor<br>Because we both must undertake to please<br>The Groundlings[229] i' the pit! |
| **MOLE:** | That's not funny, Hole. What's funny is,<br>That we're in the same Union. I always thought so.<br>I brought it up at meetin' last night . . . |
| **HOLE:** | Don't lumber me with Labor talk! But heave<br>That box o' bones up here, for the Plague goes on! |
| **MOLE:** | Then we are like to Ushers in God's Globe,[230]<br>Fer we must turn o'er the crowd, and clear<br>The Boxes, and make room for Late arrivals! |

*ENTER EDMUND, distracted.*

| | |
|---|---|
| **ED:** | Ho there! Good Constables of Death![231] |
| **HOLE (*ASIDE*):** | 'Tis abdicated Edmund. |
| **MOLE:** | What? Still 'ere, m'lord? |
| **HOLE:** | Doff thy wig and gravel at his feet, Mole! |
| **ED:** | Canst tell me where, along these Silent avenues,<br>These tracts of marble Homes, |

---

[229] A rival acting troupe, working the streets of Holy Wood. They would often visit the Globe Theatre and act as a claque, laughing at the wrong places.

[230] Wm Shakespheare's own theatre-in-the-round, the Globe was probably the site of AYWT's first performance in 1605.

[231] The Constables of Death was a powerful guild, not unlike The Congress of Grave Makers and Coarse Actors (see note 221, above). The Constables primary responsibility was to insure that the individual within the coffin was truly there and not "golde-bricking," the common practice of loading a coffin with a corpse-weight of bricks, while the assumed dead man was free to start a new life in a different clime, leaving his family and debtors behind. The Constables examined the corpse for signs of life and certified that some other stiff had not replaced the putative deceased. Thus the phrase "stiffing the systeme." The Constables' contribution to civil order was celebrated by the notorious rhymester, Bogart Falcone:
"The fun'ral bells do solemn sound,/Another soul is in the ground.
But none shall find that final rest/Until their vitals pass the test
By Constables Of Death who scan/The corpse and see if it's the man
Whose name is on yon grave stone writ/Or is that shroud a counterfeit?"
From Thrustmorton Geespot, *The Revels and Ribalds of Bogart Falcone*, Haynanny Press, Bedlam, 1876

|         | These Golden Arches[232]
Resides my late pal, Ned?[233] |
| ------- | ----------------------------- |
| HOLE:   | Address him 'ere, within this very
Oaken Box, yer Grace. |
| MOLE:   | We've fresh evicted him from
Out his sunken living room.[234] |
| ED:     | Then open me the door to his retreat, good Worms,
That I might a Relic take, a Token
Of our Friendship past. |
| HOLE:   | Nay, sir. We cannot now begin a coffin-break,
For yon Great Clapper[235] signals soon a Union
    Lunch for Clowns and Clods alike.
Let's off, Mole. |
| MOLE:   | I will be off. |
| HOLE:   | Come on, then! |
| MOLE:   | I'm going off. . . . I'm almost off. . . . I'm off. |

*EXEUNT Gravediggers.*[236]

---

[232] A traditional grave decoration in the Hoch Pflegmlican Church liturgy.

[233] Researchers have speculated endlessly on the "Ned Question." Happenstance sarcastically mocks Stormendrain about sleeping "in bed, with Ned," in *AYWT* I, ii. Edmund speaks affectionately to "pretty" Ned, now dead (of the war or of the plague?) here. Are we meant to assume the Neds are the same? And if so, what questions might this raise in the light of the Elizabethan practice of casting young men in the roles of female characters like "Marie?" See Pagliacci, Camille, *Soliloquize Dirty To Me*, Radon Press, Solilicon Valley, California, 1993. And is not "Ned" simply an affectionate name for "Edmund?"

[234] The Pflegmish littoral is below sea level, guarded by a bevy of sturdy dykes. Unfortunately, the conjunction of the full Moon with the Vernal Equinox induces The Virgin Flush, a tide so strong that no wall can contain it. The clay feet that support the Pflegmish homes are regularly washed away, sinking the domiciles many meters into the mud. The Pflegmers accommodated themselves to this style of semi-sunken living which in time produced the Mold Plagues that decimated the population until the advent of Neige Jaune (later canonized as St. Lysole) who produced a simple anti-molding agent from stale urine and dust bunnies. AS

[235] God was often seen as applauding the efforts of the playwright in those days, even as King James himself was said to be a great fan of the theatres.

[236] See "*Hole*" — *Every Inch An Actor*, in *Annals of Infinite Research*, Oct-Dec 1984 Special Issue, edited by Knewt Gingrell.

| ED: | The happy lumps! They jest as if to say
That Death's not real. What is reality?[237]
'Tis but this realty, bought for such an awful Price,
And subdivided thus, but six-by-six-by three.
And where's the room for me?
Royalty, sans realty.
I'd stay. Yet go I must.
If I lived here with Ned, I'd never leave,
For I'd be home by now.
Knock, knock! Who's there? What, Ned?
Still dead? Come! Let me pull thy leg,
An' I will show thee Norway![238]
What times we'll have! I'll talk,
You'll lend an ear. There's still one left.
I'll fill your empty skull with drink,
And toast a skoal to ev'ry Midnight Schoolgirl
That I see.
What say you, pretty Ned? Nothing? No thing?
No thing thou art — 'tis fitting, thou shouldst
Speak so soft. And yet, I'll hear thee. |
|---|---|

*EDMUND listens.*

| MARIE: | Edmund? |
|---|---|
| EDMUND: | Ah! I hear thee! |

*ENTER MARIE, enhampered with her boxed luncheon.*

| MARIE: | Why sit thee in that box
And play thus with thy bone, my Lord? |
|---|---|
| EDMUND: | Why, coz Marie! |

---

[237] Probably the most often quoted of *AYWT*'s famous speeches, this meditation on the meaning of Death struck Thoreau as "the chiefest reason for my building a cabin in the Pond" (in *Journal of a Walk to Mnt. Morednek*, 1844).

[238] Sir Larry Oliver got a lot out of this speech by playing with his bone. That is, Ned's leg bone, which he used to knock on the casket and, once, when infatuated with Marlon Brando, brandished erotically and ad libbed, "Let's hike to Norway! Or better still, I'll call you on my bonophone. It's such a local call!"

**MARIE:**
*"Why sit thee in that box and play thus with thy bone, My Lord?"*

**MARIE:** Come, I've a Box for thee — 'tis filled with
Sweetest Meats and butter'd Buns.[239]
I've love-crossed Clams[240] and French-style
Jelly Roll.[241]
Let's pick a crypt and spread
A checkered cloth
And lay us down to eat.

**EDMUND:** What sudden appetite inspires thee thus
To spread thy Dainties[242] out
Upon this Hallow'd Ground?

**MARIE:** A last sup, my lord.

**EDMUND:** Alas.

**MARIE:** And I would your St. Judas be,
Thus to kiss thee off.

**EDMUND:** By that account, my Nunc' the Count
Would thus St. Peter be,
For he has bid me now three times adieu,
E'er Chanticleer arose.

**MARIE:** I've a budding rose or three myself, my Lord.
And Chanticleer as well. That Cock will rise
No more[243] — his breast lies Broasted

---

[239] A veiled reference to "The Buttered Bums," twin cabin boy clowns who make merry in the Fyre Sygne's unpublished, "A Travail Rounde The Worlde." For more, see Casey Frybummer, *Round Tales In A Flat World* (Solid State Press, Chillicothe, 1970)

[240] Mollusk, *Labium Rockefellerensis.*

[241] Chef Crockett *ibid already*, assembles his "Honeymoon Breakfast" from these items.

[242] Undergarments.

[243] Pierre, the Baron Chanticleer (dubbed "Pete The Cock" by his London detractors) was the last of his Norman clan to pretend to the English throne. The Baron's claim to the crown dates back to his ancestor Remi Le Batard, conceived on the battlefield at Hastings by William The Conqueror and his loyal camp follower, Charlotte Chanticleer (later the Duchess of Earl after her marriage to King Speedo of Checkershire). For two centuries the Chanticleers promoted the myth that William had penned an alternate will on his deathbed designating Le Batard's son Clarence Henry as his rightful heir. "Pete The Cock" came to an untimely end on the wrong end of his boar spear during a truffle hunt on his entailed estate, Prix Fixe. AS

|          | In my hamper here, with Bangers<br>Drown'd in Beer.[244] |
|----------|--|
| EDMUND:  | Thy tempting tongue doth het me up!<br>Yet, ghastly orders from my Holy Father's Ghost<br>Oblige me take this food to go. |
| MARIE:   | Had I reveal'd such flesh to thee<br>As that apparent apparition show'd to me,<br>You'd not run off, but stop and et it here. |
| EDMUND:  | Speake't thou of Communion,<br>Dear virgin Maid?[245] |
| MARIE:   | Come, pray! That I might be thy Host<br>That thou could'st take me 'pon your Tongue. |
| EDMUND:  | I've the Blood for it, if you've the Wine! |
| MARIE:   | Within my unspoil'd chalice,<br>Let's Transubstantiate.[246] |
| EDMUND:  | T' Hell with that! Let's do it here! |
| MARIE:   | In Hallow'd ground, my Lord? |
| EDMUND:  | Fear not. I'll rise like Lazarus,[247]<br>Uncorrupted, clean. |

---

[244] Another reference to the abortive Fawlkes attempt to blow up Parliament. The storage of the explosives in casques of beer considerably diminished, one might even say dampened their power.

[245] According to Celtic myth, all women including the most promiscuous are "virgins made" on the night of the full moon. See Wilhelm Choreboy, *The Moon Through Holly Shone* (Wringraith House, Cadbury, 1903).

[246] This entire sequence, which pokes fun by way of erotic metaphor at certain High Church rituals, was considered unreverential by the time of the Puritan Elision and was condemned outright in the Third Republic. Whigs found it particularly distasteful. The Disestablishment brought it back into favor, and today (2009) one finds such productions as Shakesphere In The Park making it the comic centerpiece of their performance. Indeed, Kevin Kline and Madonna dropped this scene from their matinees, for fear of offending the elderly.

[247] During a production of *AYWT* at Ford's Theater, with President Clinton in attendance, the leading actors (both Canadian) ad libbed: Marie: "Mr. President!" Edmund: "Let's leave this boneyard rank and stinkin'!" Marie: "And hop in the sack where once slept Lincoln!"

**MARIE:** And I shall rise, corrupted,
But a Queen.

*EXEUNT EDMUND and MARIE behind a crypt.*

*ENTER EDMUND EDMUND, armed, followed by the BISHOP.*

**ED ED:** Cretin! Creep! Croutknolled Gangrell![248]
Mousehunting Mumblecrust!
I've heard it all! Diverginating Hinderling![249]
O Chastity![250]
Thy rule is now o'er-thrown!
And gentle Hymen, split!
I must play the Goat,[251] now Edmund monkeys
With her, back to back.
My Virgin Queen! O Nunc', hast Holy Church
A cure, a salve, a splint for broken Dreams,
Now finish'd, unbegun?
I'll have them both! I'll jump upon their backs
And ride them both to Hell!
Deux is mon droit!

**[BISHOP:** Hold, course-acting boy! Put up thy naughty
Soldier's tool!

**ED ED:** Let me go!][252]

**BISHOP:** Soften your ardor, Nephew.
I have the balm you seek.

---

[248] A bird common to the Pflegmish Alps, similar to the Ruby-headed Tit, *osmosis proctori*.

[249] A reference to Lord and Lady Hinderling, much despised for their inordinate wealth, unpaid debts and odious personalities. The Elizabethan essayist, Sir Maple Bacon, calls them "two turdes afloat in the castle punchbowle." [Yuckkch, ED.)

[250] In the awesomely corrupt Great Folio, "O Son, O Chere, O Chastity!"

[251] An obvious reference to the Elizabethan practice of doubling up on parts. The actor who played Edmund Edmund must have also been enlisted to play the Goat (or Ghost) in Act II, Sc. i.

[252] In brackets is a spurious text ad libbed by "Spike" Mulligan in the Raadio Pflegm production and the retort by Sir James Keach of the RSC upon being grabbed by the lapels.

| | |
|---|---|
| **ED ED:** | That's better yet! I'll bomb them back<br>To Pflegmland's stoned age! Where is't? |
| **BISHOP:** | My soothing balm is vengeful Medicine. |
| **ED ED:** | Then let me doctor play,<br>And I'll prescribe it straight![253] |

---

[253] Edmund Edmund's claim to the throne was as bogus as Bolingbroke's. During Cromwell's reign, productions of *AYWT* ended here, deprived of the glorious Shakespherian rewrites, and continued with the following trumped up justification:

*BISHOP displays the Royal Scroll.*

| | |
|---|---|
| **BISHOP:** | It is as we suspected. You are connected by this Line<br>To King Bernardo, fountainhead of all our woes.<br>And south upon this line, direct 'wixt aged Count<br>And Dame Souse, his childhood bride.<br>There find we thee, Edmund Edmund, Duke of Earl,<br>And thence by indirection, thou art that<br>Which thou has always seem'd —<br>A Royal Bastard. |
| **ED ED:** | Then, Nuncle, I am the luckiest bastard in Pflegm.<br>But what of Edmund? |
| **BISHOP:** | Your twin brother? After Brother mine hath et his most surprising lunch,<br>I'll call thee Count. |
| **ED ED:** | You'll call me not a Count when I'm a Duke. By Dad! You'll call me King,<br>and set a throne upon my head! |
| **BISHOP:** | You're flushed with power! Be not heady, lest thou be headless.<br>For yet a single thing alone stands between your getting all the<br>head that you deserve. |
| **ED ED:** | Aye! Edmund! |
| **BISHOP:** | Here comes the Count and his Montage!<br>Let's off to lunch, 'twill launch us all. |

So was the play abridged throughout the dreary Roundhead Days, so psychically distressing was the heady concept of hereditary morality. The next line of the comedy was, of course, "What a wonderful supper!" (*Que bellissimna foccacia!*), the traditional opening line of every Milanese *commedia*, declaimed by the actor with the largest Stuffed Cod Piece (see *Ibid, who has left the room*).

**BISHOP:** Yes, yes! But wait! Choke back thy ardor.
Creep with me within yon family Crypt,
Where, like two 'pothecaries we will write
Their Soul's release in our most Aweful Script.

*EXEUNT, THEN A doleful Consort of MUSICK.*

*"All the shores were glitch'd and gloomy,
Broad-leaf'd land of mighty Roi-Tan."
Buster Artunian as Edmund Edmund
in Barbeque Classics' All Canyon Tour (1973).*

# ANYTHYNGE YOU WANT TO
## Acte Four, Scene One

*The Throne Room of the Castle Pflegm. A Brass Fanfare.*

*The cheering of the COURT is heard off-stage.*

**A VOICE:** Huzzah! Huzzah!
Bernardus Rex Secundum!
Ars Gratia Artis![254]

*ENTER FANGBONER, with a Steward.*

**FANG:** The King is crowned at last!
Break out the wine, Steward.

**STEWARD:** I am broke out, sir. 'Tis the plague.[255]

**FANG:** Then in the kitchen stay and wear a waxen Nose.[256]
But send in Butts of woolly Wine
And sacks of Bully Beer.[257]
The court comes close up my behind.

---

[254] The Motto of the Pflegmish Kings.

[255] No less a scholar than Vwadek P. Marciniak in his *Politics, Humor and the Counterculture — Laughter in the Age of Decay* (Peter Lang, 2008) finds in Firesign's Seventh Seal Calvary a "brilliant reference to Ingmar Bergman's masterpiece of a film, which dealt with that (*sic*) medieval Catholic flagellants of the fourteenth century's Great Plague." In addition, he finds that Firesign's metaphorical escape from the Plague "offers new insights in the world of a logic you may have listened to on cable news or other examples of an oxymoron of reason." We couldn't agree more!

[256] In the plague years, Pflegmlanders wore wax noses, not for any protective purpose, but in order to add some kind of levity to what was otherwise an awful situation. Plagues are no joke, as is well known.

[257] A popular local brew from Ye Olde Bearwhize Brewery, est. Londern, 1556, owned by Thos. A. Burbanke.

**STEWARD:** I'll do't or die, sir. Maybe both.

*ENTER the COUNT, now King of Pflegm, attended by his Court.*[258]

**COURT:** Huzzah!

**COUNT:** Welcome, Nobles, partners all!
Projectors[259] of our new-Crowned State.
Once only Castle Pflegm, it mortgaged to the teeth
By Japanese,[260] is now, by our decree,
Imperium Pflegmaticum Presents,
And takes its rightful place of fiscal pow'r
Among the Majors and the Independents.
A Conglomerate of interests, herewith merged.
We'll take on Fortune, yet not see it splurged!

**COURT:** Huzzah!

**COUNT:** Now, to keep Eternal Peace among us all,
We'll stage an Inter-active War.
And such a Moving Picture[261]

---

**258** Evidently, when the company of actors was thin, the members of the Court consisted only of Mulholland, Fairfax and Burbank — the *troika* of communications, plumbing and beer which runs everyday life in Pflemland, even today. In fatter times, Ye Fyresygne added more players, so that the Inventory of the Admiral's Company included "cloakes fr Areguylle, Belverlie & Mel Rose, the Court." This would have been Lord Argyle, head of the McPlaid Clan, who met his death at Bestwick, impaled by a turnip. Beverly's identity is unclear. Might this refer to Princess Beverly of Prussia, a distant relative of the Earl of Essex? As for Lord Andrew (Jim) Melrose, he was a London figure of dandyism, a creature of ridicule.

**259** The Projectors, or Projectionists, voted for the Holy Pflegmish Empire's leader, in the days when there had been a Holy Pflegmish Empire — *Imperium Pflegmaticum.*

**260** Incomprehensible. A misprint for "Swisse?" AS suggests it is a garbling of "Capon's niece," and so a reference to Alona Helmsley, who inherited her uncle's banking house, Capon & Fryers, becoming the Pflegmland's principal source of loans. This crafty and insatiable woman extracted political and sexual favors as part interest on the enormous debt. Some 21st century actors ironically up-date the play here, by ad-libbing "Berkley's Bank" or "AIG."

**261** In this famous scene, perhaps the most debated of all his work, which has been nearly argued to death, Shakesphere shows us the inner workings of the Elizabethan theatre. A "Movinge Pickture" was a tableau presented by children in which they posed in representations of famous works of literature: *Pylgrimmes Progress*, or as homilies from everyday life: "Thynges looke bettre near Water." The Queen was inordinately fond of homilies, and consumed large amounts made from fried New World corn smothered in good English butter, gaining huge amounts of weight in the process. She would like to watch two or three tableaux a day, sometimes renting them from local theatres so she might repeat them, over and over. Derrick Escrow severely edited this text for the Raadio Pflegm broadcast.

> Of a War we see, that only We can frame it,
> Focuss'd in our inner eye.
> A spectacle of arms, a War to end all Debts,
> An exercise to lead us, Moses like,
> From out a Sea of Red,
> And guide our columns up to inky Black!

**FAIRFAX**[262]: You'll need stars to lead the way!
The Duke of Wayne[263] is lost! [The Don is done!
Our Ginger's gone!
Shall we depend upon a Gladiator's feeble mind?][264]

**COUNT:** We'll find new names above the titles, Fairfax.

**MULHOL**[265]: The products of this realm of late
Have not been well distributed!
I losses have sustained!

**BURBANK**[266]: The capitol tax upon the Indies's gains

---

[262] Benjamin Fairfax, later Lord Fleetstreet, was the chief gossip of Shakesphere's time. He also owned a fleet of "honeywagons, carts and vans."

[263] The Duke was a famous amateur scientist of the time, whose observations of the heavens were written up in *The Celestiale Behemoth*, by George Frundt (1601). He named the constellation "The Newt" in the rightwing sky.

[264] The text within brackets added during the Second Stars War (1690-1960). Further amendment was imposed by the Gabby Hayes Office during the second Crumbwell's heyday: "The Schwartz O'Neger's terminated/ And rules o'er a broken golden realm./Our Brokeback Ledger's no longer on the heath." O'Neger, the strong man of El Dorado, once thought invincible, was brought down by the sudden disappearance of all wealth in his country. Lord Ledger of Brokeback Heath, a strange young man, died of a potent cocktail he himself had made. It is said that after he was gone, his fellow knights assumed his identity from time to time, but no one dared replace him.

[265] The Fourth Duke of Mulholland built the Lerndon aqueduct, which piped the city's used water north to Southern Scotland. His discontent with the fees he received for the job was well-known, he later sued, and the concessions he had been promised still stand. The workmen who constructed the aqueduct would have gone on the Duke's dole had there not been a war to employ them as "extras," or cannon fodder.

[266] Thomas Alva Burbanke, briefly Lord Mayor of London, was a former Alehouse owner, doing business at the Signe of the Portly Pigge. An independent pubkeeper, Burbanke was badly hurt by the Beer & Brewing Tax of 1601 and ran for office on the sole issue of repeal. He was thrown out of office when he was found using child labor from one of his orphanages, where they were known as Burbanke's Best Boys. (See note for "Best Boys," coming up.)

|             | Done deliberate damage to our Stock.[267] |
|---|---|
| COUNT: | We hear thee, Lord Mayor Burbank, <br> Lofty Mulholland. <br> Know that we shall pledge such guarantees, <br> From all the houses in our realm, <br> That our investment will secure your safe return. |
| BURBANK: | I'm not so sure! |
| COUNT: | And, further, we will no concessions take, <br> But leave them[268] all to you! |
| MULHOL: | Right then! It's a deal! |
| COUNT: | And let us not forget to leave <br> Our Great Director's Cut to Him alone! |
| FAIRFAX: | Then let us now our comp'nies join! <br> I've Merchants, Ivory and books no one has read! |
| COUNT: | My Castle Rocks with joy at this good news. |
| BURBANK: | I've a crew of ancient Gaffers,[269] and I shall <br> My Best Boys[270] add to your supply! |
| FAIRFAX: | And I a thousand Extras more shall offer up.[271] <br> I've men who ride a horse, and if they fall, <br> They'll rise to do their Stunts again. |

---

[267] Stock was sold in these ventures by the Queen, in order to pay for her increased eating habits. Specifically, her love of a savory dish brought by her publicist, The Earl Wilson, from the New World — popcorn. A much clearer way of saying this line would be: "The tax upon the popcorn . . ."

[268] That is to say, the Popcorn Concessions, which, along with trade in immense containers of strong drink flavored with West Indian coca (!), provided fortunes to owners of various Palaces, Odeons and Music Halls around the country.

[269] Duffers. Grandsires. Also, Frogge fishermen.

[270] See the note *re* buttered buns, earlier.

[271] Extra troops — "faceless and drawn" — would cover the Count's "back end."

| | |
|---|---|
| **MULHOL:** | Sound men have I! <br> A Second Unit I'll supply. |
| **BURBANK:** | And when we come to Grips, I hold the key. |
| **COUNT:** | Thanks, studious Burbank, for throwing in thy lot. <br> A *Buena Vista*[272] do I spot![273] |
| **FAIRFAX:** | I've Honey-wagons sweet, and carts and Vans. <br> Do cry but Action, and we'll roll 'em, sire. |
| **COUNT:** | We'll shoot by Night as if it were by Day![274] <br> I've hundred Points, and so I'll give New Lines[275] <br> To ev'ry faithful Highland border-laird. <br> A Universal gesture, Paramount to none, <br> And yes, you'll more than Gold win, Mayor, <br> Lords and nobles, United Artists at The End, <br> And if this Dream Works one-two-three, <br> The Final Credits we shall live to see![276] |
| **COURT:** | Huzzah! |

*ENTER EDMUND EDMUND and The BISHOP, armed.*

---

[272] Echoing a remark Don Quixote makes, looking across La Mancha at a phalanx of attacking windmills — "*Que buena vista! Son mios!*"

[273] The prompt-books for the larger company of players used in the 18th century included the thought-provoking line: "Wilshire, Beverly, Melrose! Thy courses made concrete are parallel with ours." (It made ED' s think of a GPS-guided tour of the L.A. River. An additional line was supplied here for the company's "Froggy" speaker: "And be not *bleu*, my Liege, for I/Count Cameroon, titanic camouflage devised/ To make your *petit soldats* ten feet tall." To which the Count replied: "Our dependable old Avatar. Merci." This was the "Froggy's" only line but he also served as the Company representative ("Avatar") to the Thespis Guild.

[274] He was boasting, of course. This military tactic has only recently (1995) become available. The tragedian Sir Arthur Mucus-Bunburry, his disbelief in the idea so overwhelming, frequently reversed "night" and "day," until corrected by his Dresser.

[275] Borders. This would hopefully solve long-standing territorial disputes over almost everything having to do with them.

[276] The much diminished text recorded for Raadio Pflegm was the result of a Writers Guild dispute which found for the Lord of Holy Wood, Goofus von Katzenberg.

**ED ED:** Cut! Cut! Cut short thy speech!
I swear 'pon Holy Edward Wood,[277] thou'lt ne'er my
Director be! I'm Edmund Edmund!
Back'd by foreign Capitals,[278]
I've assets fresh unfroze from fishy
New-found lands,[279] that I may sit upon the Throne
And call the Shots!

**COUNT:** What lazy lout did dare to let this upstart
Drive in past our golden Gates?

**ED ED:** 'Twas through the greatest Agency of all
That I arrived.[280]

**BISHOP:** I[281] his soul's representative be.
Stands here before you, Edmund Edmund,
Our late brother King Bernardo's bastard Babe,
Whom out of kindness we did, in his swaddling,
Place upon a plank and push to sea.[282]

**COUNT:** I well remember.

**BISHOP:** Tender tradewinds blew him West to Indica,
Isle of fire-skinn'd, smoke-digesting cannibals.

**ED ED:** There I stay'd, and grew, and prosper'd midst
Those home-grown folk, and with my baby's beads
Did purchase that entire land for Pflegm!

---

[277] Saint Edward of the Holy Wood, reviled for wearing women's clothes, was martyred by his critics in 1152. His writings, especially *Planus Nonus Extra-Terestralis* have, surprisingly, considering the Saint's illiteracy, recently returned to favor.

[278] Norway was to have taken a bite out of Pflegm in return for its help.

[279] Trade with the "Indies" seems very much on the Royal bastard's mind.

[280] In spite of the Royal Contract, here Edmund Edmund calls upon the Church to support his claims. This line also may be a caustic reference to William & Morris, a London theatrical Agency.

[281] "I," of course, was understood to mean ICM, Latin initials for "International Chemical Monkes." The Order was created by St. Hydroginous of Lethe in 1157.

[282] This story is told and retold in different ways in Hollinshead's "Chronicles" and can be traced in one form or another to Aeschylus. In the Greek version, the Hero is tied to a "stick," and sent into a whirlpool of comely babes at sea.

**COUNT:** Well-guarded welcome, double Edmund.

**ED ED:** Once you sent me hence with but an orphan's
String of plastic Pearls. Now the favor I return,
With precious gifts like these.

**COUNT:** What's this? A cedar chest, emblazon'd
With a savage maiden's face?

**ED ED:** The gift's within.

**COUNT:** These stinking leaves?[283]

**ED ED:** The Wild Men of Indica[284] ignite them in their mouths
And suck them for a spell.

**BISHOP:** I've sulphur for a light.

**ED ED:** And while thou tak'st thy toke,
I'll lay 'ponst thee thy second gift,
The greatest one of all. A lay, entitled,
"Roi-Tan, or The Injun King's Revenge."
By me, who King shall never be.

**COUNT:** Lay on, Nephew.

**ED ED:** "All the shores were Glitched and Gloomy,
Broad-leaf'd land of mighty Roi-Tan.
Little White Owl, drew I her to me,
Injuns watching . . ."

*An Explosion.*

---

[283] Long presumed to be "cigars," rolled from Indian tobacco, authorities now disagree. Placer says they are the Native American kinnicinik, while Leary and Ott attribute the reference to the South American pharmacology of which they are so fond.

[284] These "Wild Men" were natives of the Hemp Islands, which formed a bowl at the end of the stem of the Hemp Archipelago. Unlike the other Indican tribes who fought fiercely against the Western adventurers, the Hemp Islands' residents were easily enslaved. Captain Peter Cook described the effortless subjugation of the Sensamilla tribe:
> No need for brass artillery/Or diplomatic treachery.
> So heedless, seedless were these folk/That dumbly did they don the yolk.

**COUNT:** A light! Alight! My beard's aflame!
Then, by Proxy![285] War within our Company
Must reign.

**ED ED:** Forgive me, sir. The hemp is young, like me,[286]
And went off premature.

**COUNT:** Pestio!

**PESTIO:** I'll quench thy face, White Knight,
Ere thee be Blackamoor!

**COUNT:** Away all! Fool, lead me from the room.
I'll n'er again trust gifts from Geeks[287]
That in the night go Boom![288]

*EXEUNT COURT*

*The MUSICK of a Pflegmish March.*

**ED ED:**[289] I've not the numbers now, but know, false Mogul,
That I am underwrit by Foreign sails.

---

[285] A oath-taking form of Saint Proximus, patron saint of oath-takers.

[286] The spelling "hemp" instead of the traditional "hump" makes for an interesting observation here. Hemp was well-known in the New World as well as the Old, where it was used for tying things to other things and for low-cost T-shirts. Perhaps the leaves are of this substance, although that is certainly not clear.

[287] See Uncle Rebus' *Roamin' History of the World*, Restoration Press, N. J., where the Geeks are referred to as "an uninformed people who ate themselves and thus were seen no more."

[288] "Going boom" was a nautical term meaning "go forward," that is, toward the boom of the ship. Geek maritime enterprises of the time used galleons with booms to extend trade all the way to Sweden. Had they had rudders, not a few of them might have returned.

[289] A longer speech is found in Quarto XX, probably written by an actor wishing for a speech as long as Edmund's:
Now let me think, though thinking's not my game.
I long to fight, and yet for all I've killed,
The lid's not mine, nor am I King as yet.
The former wimpled sands now shine with thirty-weight
And atomizing towers foul smoke the reaches of the sky.
Our native Pflegm she weeps, she bleeds with war,
Her chimneys are blown down, they say, and horses

> And I, this very night, shall be prepared to fight,
> For I delight in Action![290]

*MARTIAL MUSIC Playes On and On*

> They do dine one on t'other. S' good, it's strange.
> There are heard weird screams of death and awful hags
> Groan out their prophesies o'er bones of Spanish fowl.
> I like this world, I swear it suits my darkened moods.
> All's well, someone has said, that soon will end. Well.

A further addition, handwritten in the margins of the 1606 broadside edition, seems to be the work of a actor explaining himself to the company:

> My vengeful Uncle Nuncle fumes and spews.
> He flames with ancient Psyche's babbling tongues.
> He spreads his poison rumors all about,
> How I'm conspiring 'gainst his life and self.
> O gentle Frawd, come forth and give him peace,
> Damp down his spirits as water under grease.
> Wrap up his batter'd ends of nerves
> And give him pow'r to see:
> His enemy's inside himself —
> It's certainly not me.

**290** "Action!" was the traditional cry of activists in the Indie Wars.

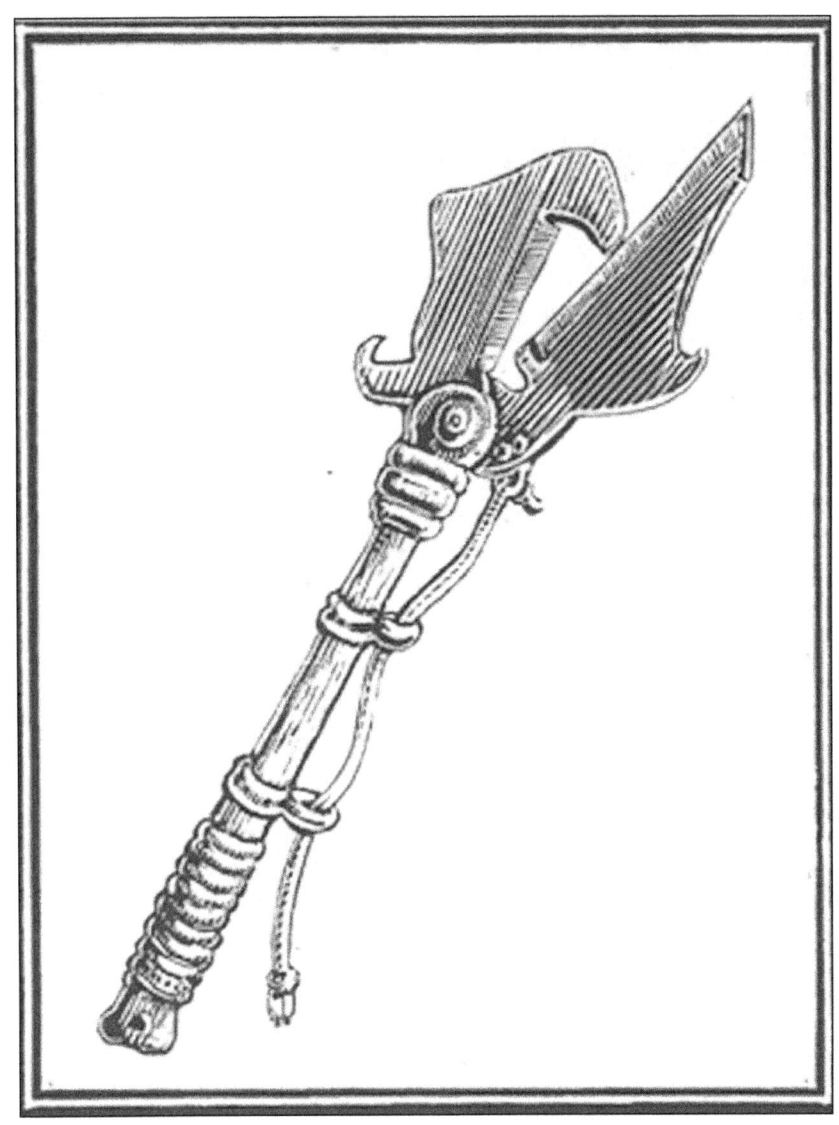

### "KURDMANGLER"
*Early device for squeezing the milk of human kindness out of strangers.*
*Used originally against the one-man invasion of Nurd the Kurd (1127 AD), this loathsome invention was subsequently fitted with Multiple Independently Targetable Reentry Vehicles and stands high in the Pflegmish Royal Navy's arsenal of powerful obsolete weapons.*
*Recreation by Bruce Litz.*

# ANYTHYNGE YOU WANT TO
## ACTE FOUR, SCENE TWO

*The Field of BATTLE. Dead and wounded, etc. Horns of Cavalry.*

ENTER GRAPESHOT and MUZZLE, two Soldiers.[291]

| | |
|---|---|
| **GRAPE:** | Blood! Blood! All is Blood! <br> The lascivious Traitor[292] looses <br> Clouds of Spanish flies[293] at us — <br> We swat them flat! |
| **MUZZLE:** | Ho! Corporal Grapeshot! |
| **GRAPE:** | Able Muzzle! Give us thy report. |
| **MUZZLE:** | The rebel Bishop did bring a string <br> Of Popish garlic-eaters,[294] <br> Which our brave lads did chew asunder <br> And spat out upon the ground. <br> Stand the Irish strong! |
| **GRAPE:** | Thy Breadth proclaims it! Pray, <br> Stand the Irish back! And say, <br> Who led the charge? |

---

**291** The part of "Muzzle" was a favorite of Sir Henry Bloomsday, known to his myrid fans as "The Great Shenannigan," who was, from 1907 to 1924, the leading Coarse actor at Dublin's famous Crabby Theatre. (He's not, of course, to be confused with Edwin Shenannigan, the Nineteenth Century actor-manager, whose famous New Variorum Edition of 1898 forms the basis for the present text.)

**292** An oblique reference to the usurpation of the Pflegmish House Royal by the "populist" Gnutte Grinch in 1499.

**293** *Muscus toreadorum.* These vicious insects, if accidentally eaten, cause satyriasis.

**294** The politically incorrect language of these and other lines have caused *AYWT* to be characterized as "sexist and racist" by the National Council of Faculty Heads and banned on most American campuses.

MUZZLE: The Master of the Charge was Berkeley,[295] sir.
The needy King did bank on him,
And he gives credit to us all![296]

GRAPE: Look you, here come the sour, cabbage-headed Krauts,[297] to knock their worst!
Muster up hot blood! We will cold slaughter make,
And shred them first![298]

MUZZLE: Have at them!

GRAPE: Gezundheit!

*Exeunt. The Battle Rages.*

*ENTER EDMUND EDMUND, Armed and astride his Mount.*

ED ED: I'm at the Top of this Sweet Spot.
Now, Double Edmund, look you down
Into yon wooded Bowl. A Basin
Drown'd with Milky Smoke,
Encompassing the Product of your Puff'd
Desires! War and pestilence reign there,
As gaily colored Worms themselves do Loop
Through rotting Fruits of Death.
I smile, and eat of it until I'm done.
I rise, fulfilled with Nothing,
And rush to Bloody Work![299]

---

[295] Lord Berkeley, serving as exchequer to King Enery, won the Battle of Bankside (1366) by out-bidding the weapons-making cartel. Berkeley's Bank was a major holder in Pflegmish AAA Mud Bonds, until the conversion to Euros.

[296] Well, not exactly. The ability to give credit depends on the ill-known "Texas Ratio," a mathematical expression of bad loans and 90-day delinquencies divided by tangible equity plus loan loss reserves. Possibly, "a nerdy King?"

[297] A derisive Pflegmish term for the neighboring Lumpen Deutch.

[298] Chef Crockette offers "Uncle Nudinudo's Hot Sausage" in his delightful *A Battlefield Picnic* (Ch. Scribbler's Sons, New York, 1945).

[299] Derrick Escrow used this speech to great advantage in his award-winning commercial for Froot-Loops. Mel Gibson recites it while eating a bowl of the cereal.

*ENTER MARINARA, armed.*

MAR: Hey, Boss! Let's go!
Your Company, she's overspent!
You lose the light![300]

ED ED: Thanks, red-fac'd Marinara,
Faithful Keeper of the Books.

MAR: Ciao.[301]

*EXIT MARINARA, Chas'd by a Bomb.*

ED ED: He's dead. Who cares?[302]
This Golden Time[303] will bring us luck.
Each extra Soldier's worth is Three!
Cry Speed! And take it one more time![304]
Thus Full Close Up on *Gloria*[305] will I be!

*MUSIC of Martial Pipes.*

---

[300] Careful readers will note that in spite of claims to have the weapons to "shoot by night as if by day," Fr. Marinara, the over-taxed Keeper of the Books (a high ideological position in the Church of Pflegm) announces it is nearly Sunset.

[301] "Good bye."

[302] "Dead accountants tell no tales." A common medieval attitude.

[303] Again, a reference to the waning rays of the setting sun.

[304] Memorably in the Olivier *Henry V*.

[305] "His glorious swan song," according to the German cinema director Oskar von Lubitch who directed a silent version of the Franz Lehar operetta based on this play, *Die Dopplebruder aus Pflem*.

*"I'd rather call thee Brother."*
*Sir Jack Feelgood as the Count*
*at Playhouse-on-the-Eye, Lerndon 2000*

# ANYTHYNGE YOU WANT TO

## ACTE FIVE, SCENE ONE[306]

*Within the Bishop's Battle Tent.*

*MUSICK for a Dancing Girl.*

*The BISHOP reclines upon a Divan. ISIS[307] concludes her Dance.*

**BISHOP:** Bravo! Bravo!
I want to taste your Spicy Salome[308] again!
Like Holy John Baptismo,[309] I've lost my head
Upon your undulating abdomen.

**SOLDIER (OFF):** Hola! Hola! Your Grace!

**BISHOP:** Knock not upon the tent! The dust! The dust!
Sweet *Isis*, take up thy veil.
'Twill raise a flap if you don't do the same,
And disappear.

---

[306] This entire scene is spurious, having been written by an unknown hand hundreds of years after Shakesphere lived. Derrick Escrow, however, considered it to be his "Third Act," and necessary to the "dramatic arc" of the Raadio Phlegm broadcast. Absurdly, this scene ends the play without bloodshed! Where is the original Fifth Act?

[307] Elizabethan England had a shortage of Greek restaurants (indeed, England had no restaurants at all before the 1920s) and thus no "Dance of the Seventh Veil." Veil dancing itself was considered witchcraft.

[308] Probably a misprint for "salami," a veiled reference to the Royal's dubious sexual preferences.

[309] A real person (1333?-1371), though not Holy in the traditional sense. Rather, this man, born into the middle poor class in the shantytown of Bent-on-Sludge, was known simply as John (or Yawn), a name he gave himself while pouring ale over his head at an outdoor music festival, thus inventing "self-baptism" or "BeBop." For this, he was severely reprimanded by the local Abbot, Fr. Costello, who cheesed him to death with a Swiss punch, thus making him "Holey in the Sight of God."

*EXIT the Dancing Girl.*

**BISHOP:** My prayers are done. I pray you enter now.

*ENTER Soldier.*

**SOLDIER:** Will your Grace a meeting take with Don La Brea,
Duke of La Cienega, who lathered comes
From fair Castile?

**BISHOP:** Bar him not.

*ENTER a MAN, disguised as the Duke.*[310]

**"DUKE":** Good Cheer, Padre. I've beat a dead horse
All the night to meet with you.

**BISHOP:** I know you not, Dreft Duke.
I think your title does not wash.

**"DUKE":** I'll scrub then this disguise, and thou canst
Call me King.

**BISHOP:** I'd rather call thee "Brother."

*The "DUKE," taking off his disguise, is revealed as The COUNT.*

**COUNT:** So, fratern'ly, I'll speak conciliation.

**BISHOP:** Oh, really?

**COUNT:** And an end to escalating strife that threatens
To destroy us both.

**BISHOP:** What treaty could thou possibly propose?

**COUNT:** When warring brothers raise their stakes,
Lest Civil War be fought,

---

[310] The real Duke from Castile proved a washout in the soap business as people of his time had no use for washing. Washing was considered witchcraft.

|              | 'Tis better they lay down their hands
And divvy up the pot. |
|---|---|
| **BISHOP:** | Wise words.[311] |
| **COUNT:** | Kinsman, ere our young Kingdom's
Torn asunder, like wisest Solomon,
I submit we cut the child in half. |
| **BISHOP:** | Divide our blessed land? Split up this mound
Of em'rald Pflegm?[312] Separate the neighbor
From his neighbor's wife? Chop up the livers
Of this body politic? Sounds good! |
| **COUNT:** | I thought it would. You have my hand. |
| **BISHOP:** | And mine.
Now brother, having shook, a shaky Peace
We've made. And so can you.
You've but to visit the Oasis through the back. |
| **COUNT:** | I'll enter any way I can, could I but rest. |
| **BISHOP:** | The rest is up to her. |
| **COUNT:** | Ah ha! I catch thy meaning!
And so I'll catch the moment,
Praying it be all I catch tonight.
I'll this eve in Oriental splendor spend.
This Peace shall start with such a lovely end.[313] |

*EXIT the COUNT. EDMUND EDMUND enters, armed.*

**ED ED:** Cretin! Creep! Croutknolled Gangrell!

---

[311] They ought to be. The Count is quoting from the Greek philosopher Euripadeez' tragedy "The Eumenadeez."

[312] Another veiled reference, this one to the brief occupation of Hoch Pflegm by a disoriented troop of Irish mercenaries (or, by some accounts, actors) who besieged the town hall for hours until hot whiskey was poured on them from the battlements. See *Toddy Shenannigan's Barmaid's Guide*, Pickled Press, N.Y., 1898.

[313] Another reference to Isis, who has been observed by the Count as she exited, shedding her final veil.

BISHOP: Gutenaben,[314] Double Edmund.

ED ED: Mousehunting Mumblecrust!
I've heard it all! Diverginating Hinderling![315]
You two have sold me out of Crown
And country both! I'll skewer two craven
Capons 'pon this single spit!

BISHOP: Hold, coarse-acting boy![316] If you but wait,
You've only me to gut.

*The Dancing MUSICK ends abruptly.*

COUNT (*OFF*): Isis! Isis! I cease! (*He dies.*)[317]

BISHOP: He live'd to ride astride the saddle of Affairs,
And, fittingly, expires he thereon.

ED ED: And so, I'm King! At last!
The Royal Bastard's King!

BISHOP: And I, thy Churchy agent, kneel before thee,
To fit thee with thy sacred Hat.[318]

ED ED: Get down![319]

---

314 A reminder, if one was needed, that in King Richard's day, the state was run by Count Henrich von Kissenburger.

315 Edmund Edmund here displays an astonishing knowledge of Pflegmish birdlife. Both the Gangrell and Hinderling are insultingly awkward flightless animals who live on salt flats North of The Runns. The Mumblecrust, as its name indicates, is a small, dust-colored bird who lives in the thatch or attic and eats out of both house and home.

316 Referring to the crude, unschooled emoting of "local talent" who often were hired "to lend an atmosphere" to touring performances by the trained actors from Oxnard and Clambridge.

317 How convenient! Offstage sex was unlike Shakespeare. Another indication that this text, supposedly discovered by Rick Shakespeare in a shipwrecked galleon, is a total fabrication.

318 Frank Zappa made this pose famous on a widely-sold late 1960s poster.

319 Meaning, of course, bow before him and acknowledge him King of Pflegm.

We'll borrow more and fight until we're broke!

**BISHOP:** The battle scene is done.
The troops are wrapp'd[320] and gone.
Now the true work of thy Kingly office
Doth commence.

**ED ED:** Work?

**BISHOP:** Tomorrow morning, six o'clock,
Three ministers of Fiscal Finance you shall see.
At seven, a delegation you'll receive of
Oily Fisher folk, their sullen grievances to hear.
At eight, the Vet'rans of the Swabian Crusade[321]
And Mothers of the Leper's March[322] will come
To pin a rose on thee. At half-past-ten,
You'll eat.

**ED ED:** At least there's food.

**BISHOP:** There's Jellied Mold[323] and Hotel Salad,[324]
Turkish rolls and Fowl a la King.[325]

**ED ED:** This, the schedule of a chicken King!
I cannot, will not do't! I'd rather Savage be,
And with my red-hued Princess White Owl[326] live,
Happy so in sylvan anarchy. I'll go!

---

[320] "wrapp'd" = dead, ready for burial.

[321] Since none returned alive from that engagement, this can be considered an ironic reference.

[322] Another example of "Black" or "Plague" Comedie (we once would have said "sick") which laid audiences in the aisle (from which they had to be removed by Ushers from the Order of the Black Cross) in Shakespheare's time.

[323] Chef Croquette, as you would *ibidly* expect, includes these dainties in his *Cooking For Idiots*, Jinx Publishing, TX, 2000.

[324] "Steamed for days over hot water." Often, with added milk.

[325] See Creamed Cocks 'n' Croissants for Fifty, inevitably *ibid*.

[326] Possibly mythical? In the Old World, Adam's wife "Evita."

>           I'll drop the heavy Lid of State, and thusly
>           Write me out:
>             "All the shores were glitched and gloomy,
>             Stood the red man waiting for me.
>             I'll explain her swelling Belly,
>             If her Father listens to me!"

*EXIT EDMUND EDMUND.*[327]

**BISHOP:** Now, all Rule is blown away, and in the vacuum
Let Alchemy be king! I'll construct a Tower
Whose Art shall challenge Babylon!
New Adams I shall form, their Rods more
Powerful than Moses' Staff,[328] whose Force
Will permeate the Mass, and, Radiant,
Mutate all the World 'till Kingdom come!
Mercenaries, ho! Follow me, blind fellows,
You'll know me by the Glow![329]

*The BISHOP EXITS. EDMUND ENTERS.*

**EDMUND:**[330] Marie?
Where are you, Sweet Marie?
Surprise!
An empty tent? Damme, sir, she's slipped away
Once more. She plays with me,
The cunning child. What ho?

---

327 "And goode riddance!" Francis Bacon, in his satire "Who Could Want It?" Dr. Firesign's Theatre of the Plains amused red-neck audiences in Texas around 1900 by interpolating:
>   ED ED:    I'll drop this fancy accent and thusly write me out. Come on, Cheney, we're goin' ta Crawford!
>   BISHOP:   Hee haw! I'll hunt a duck, and in that blind, I'll shoot a friend!"

The idea that anybody would choose to go to the God-Forsaken Desert around Crawford was then unthinkable and a source of hoots and hollers. "Dick" Cheney was a blind torturer and terrorist whose armed mercenaries threatened at one time to control the Western Bush country. It took a village to "weed out the poison'd Bush," but Cheney escaped to an undisclosed location.

328 Aka The Elders of Zion.

329 This speech was supposedly quoted by physicist Robert Oppenheimer upon witnessing the first Atomic explosion.

330 Where has Edmund been since before the end of Act 3? With Marie? Why did he not take part in the coronation? The War? Did an actor suddenly become ill or quit the Company? Alas, no one knows.

> I hear my belle Marie! I come, I come!
> And so to knock upon thy Fam'ly Tree!

*EDMUND discovers his Nuncle's Corpse.*

**EDMUND:** What's this? My Nuncle Count? He's out!
He's stiff as he can be, and dead as Vaudeville.[331]
O sneaky Death, to nip him like a Glass of Budd![332]
How flat, Scruggs and unpotable seem to me
All the ails of this World. He's gone![333]
She's gone! And only I am left,
Who took a nap a Fool[334] and woke a King.
But King of what? I need some friends.
And we shall jointly to our Nation's
Tattered standards make amends,
And share the burthen of my unseasonable rule.
Power? I'll hand it to the People.[335]
Let them wield the Tool. And Policy?
My Policy, a plan untried as yet, but true.
Not just "Do This," or "Don't do that!"

---

[331] In other words, eternal. Compte Veau d'Ville, a singer, juggler and expert mime, was replaced as a popular entertainer by Lucian DeZi who performed in people's homes.

[332] Another Bearwhiz Brewery specialty, Budd was concocted of fresh Thames water and little else.

[333] Compare with the speech delivered by Edmundo in "Il Conde," which leads directly to his resolve to take revenge. The final ten lines have been debated by scholars since they first appeared. Some believe it to be simply a crowd-pleaser, in the manner of the 19th century's penchant for "happy endings." Others see it as a quasi-revolutionary cry for a true political overhaul in a sundered country, split between the right-wing Paartien der Nein (PDN) and left-leaning Kommucrat Paartien (KP). Not surprisingly, supporters of Barack Obama were wont to interpolate "Yes, we can!" in a stage whisper during the Campoon of 2008. In productions with no Marie, a line borrowed from Fletcher's "Dynasty of Bushies" has been substituted here: "The potted Bush is rooted out."

[334] Wait! Perhaps Edmund has been present throughout the latter scenes of the play, masquerading as Pestio, the Court Fool. On the other hand, given the example of "Midsummer Night's Dream," when a Fool takes a nap, strange things happen. Perhaps poor Edmund awakes, enters the scene with an ass's head and simply continues to make a Fool of himself.

[335] A slogan picked up by the Panthers, Hippies and Diggers at the first Love-In, who found it in the Whole Earth Catalog, where it obviously referred to beta-testing environmentally-approved gardening equipment. Originally, "giving a hand to the people" meant a gratuitous and self-serving cant used by politicians.

But "Anything You Want To!"³³⁶

*So Endeth the Plague of 'ANYTHYNGE YOU WANT TO.'*

**_BEGONE! FAREWELL!_**

---

**336** A political strategy so loony as to commit Edmund to that special madhouse reserved for Heads of State. The, let's call it for what it is, *anarchy* proposed here is more appropriate to the laid-back, "stoner," "yes, you can be" life-style of a Southern California beach-bum and so-called "treasure seeker" like Rick Shakespeare than a true Elizabethan monarch. See the Appendix.

*"Not just do this or don't do that, But Anythynge You Want To!"
Wiggan Cuppe as EdmundOh! in Blanque Cheque Theatre's
"Stupid Shakespeare!" (1979)*

# THE APPENDICES

## Further Theatricals, Recipes and Adventures with

# THE LEGENDARY FIRESIGN THEATRE
## ENTER HERE ····▶

# The Firesign Theatre

# "WAITING FOR THE MOUNT OF COUNTY CRISCO,"
## With Someone Like Him

### As Proudly Presented By
# The FIRESIGN THEATRE

**A One-Act Play in Five Acts,
Three AGAINST Nature and Four Against THE STATE
Based on the *Comedia del'arte* Classic
"'Sperate il conde di Monte Cristo"
and
A BURLESQUE of Anon's Notorious and Tragical
"Philip, Prince of Norway"**

"Let the plague begin!"

The Milanese *comedia* classic, "'*Sperate il conde di Monte Cristo,*" has inspired comedians from Moliere and the Marx Bros. to the Four or Five Crazee Guys. It has everything! Mistaken identities, dueling, violent deaths, ghosts — in short all that a bloodthirsty Sixteenth (or Twenty-First) century audience could want. No less a genius than Wm. Shakesphere used this silly play as a basis for his lost comedie "Anythynge You Want To."[337] For the following text, translated and edited especially for this volume by scholar, treasure-hunter and party-hound Rick Shakespeare, many dialectical versions have been collated into a dramatic whole. Traditional stage directions have been added in brackets by the Editor.

## "WAITING ON THE MOUNT OF COUNTY CRISCO"

**PETER:** Thank you, President Furburger, Admiral Groat, honored Doctors, and Bunkmates. Tonight we proudly prevent "Waiting For The Mount of County Crisco, With Someone Like Him."

**PHIL P:** To be performed by a large cast in short pants and five acts — three of them against nature . . .

**PHIL A:** Two of them against the State . . .

**PETER:** We'll be back with more Sports in just a minute, but first . . .

**PHIL A:** The Scene! The darkened mind of pre-Renaissance Man, somewhere in France, a week ago Tuesday.

**DAVID:** Let the plague begin![338]

---

[337] In their generally interesting, although ill-researched "Preface" to TFT's *Big Mystery Jukebox* (Straight Error Press, 1974), Gemstone and Yucamoto date "Anythynge You Want To" to the year 1605. Authorship has subsequently been positively established by a computer project at SSU begun in 1977 to 1568 and the brothers Shakesphere (sometimes called "Shakespierre"), a villainous band of plagiarists and scene stealers who actually rewrote a turgid Latin "boy's play," "*Mons Christus Contendo,*" adapting it to their own scandalous purposes. That play, turgidly translated by Canon W. Kneebone LFC as "The Struggle for Christ's Mountain," in the *Journal* of the Old Play Society, Oxford, Summer 1914, can best be described as a doggerel account of a man's life-long encounters with terrifying symbolic figures. Why TFT ascribes their stage version of a corrupt chancel play to the *commedia* or *Anon.* traditions can not be explained. [ED]

[338] Later, Firesign developed a less stupid opening in which the Prologue (DO) proclaimed:
While on your asses, warming up the seats,
Admit me Prologue to this dreadful piece —
And find no cause to leave, for doors are barred

*[ENTER IL CONDE (DO), with him IL CARDINALE (PB) and EDMUNDO (PP).[339]]*

CONDE: What a wonderful supper![340]

CARDINALE: How liked you the field pie,[341] bro'?
'Twas of mine own hand made.

CONDE: I liked it but a bit, and so a bitty bite I took,
And passed it by.

CARDINALE: (*ASIDE*) Rare!

*[EDMUNDO DUO (PA)[342] appears in the traditional ventalone, or "stage window."]*

ED DUO: Well done!

CARDINALE: (*ASIDE*) And, by the by,
If bite of poison'd pie's enough,
Then by and by, he'll bye-bye be.

---

Behind thine unsuspecting feets!
So suckers all, we'll succor and we'll haunt you
With this our play, called ANYTHYNGE YOU WANT TO.
But! Lo and Hi! Here comes good Marster Pedro — say!
He'll cry out "Uncle! Uncle!" at the last,
But at the first our Nuncle he'll portray.
A vile man, and in his vial he keeps a viper hid,
To do in Edmund, orphan Count, yet no Count's kid.
(Count the Counts as we proceed, it's no account to me!)
Who's he?! Tis him! No, no, indeed tis not!
But how his darksome mien and mean demeanor mean
But trouble, I know not — and yet, I needs proceed
To play the Ancient Lord — and leave the stage to these!

[339] Traditional *comedia* characters, "Il Conde" was distinguished by a pointed beard and three-cornered hat; "Il Cardinale" by a red robe and hooked nose; "Edmundo" was, of course, the *innocente*, who always wore an ill-fitting wig and carried an out-sized flagon.

[340] The familiar *commedia* opening line. The 1977 FT performances developed the drama between the "Count" and the "Bishop" to a spectacular excess. See "Act V" at the end of this script.

[341] Original, *pizza di cavallo*.

[342] In Milanese *comedia*, the *Gemello* or "Twin," was a trickster and pervayor of fun. He would often dress in women's clothes and pretend to be *La Colombina*.

| | |
|---|---|
| **ED DUO:** | What? |

*[EDMUNDO DUO disappears behind the traditional arassio, or stage curtain, and the CARDINALE EXITS]*

| | |
|---|---|
| **EDMUNDO:** | Nuncle! |
| **CONDE:** | Nephew! |
| **EDMUNDO:** | Gezundtheit![343] |
| **CONDE:** | Grazie bitte. |
| **EDMUNDO:** | Your Niece, my cousin, refused me entrance<br>To your room! I fought her to a draw!<br>I hear you are ailing. Well, so am I! |

---

[343] Original, Nanno! Nono! Nuncio!

*[HE DRINKS.]*

**CONDE:** Would that wenching were your bitter brew.
Alas! I fear that poysenberry pie[344] I et
Will bury me.
'Tis always thus. My reverend brother
Hastens o'er to spice my soup
Or add a dose of some odd herb into my glass.
But now, methinks, he's play'd the cook,
And both my life and kingdom he has took.
And so, Edmundo, e're I slip into that
Biggest sleep of sleeps, that naweful yawning gape
From which there's ne'er return . . .

**EDMUNDO:** O Nuncle! *[He yawns]* Speak not of yawning!

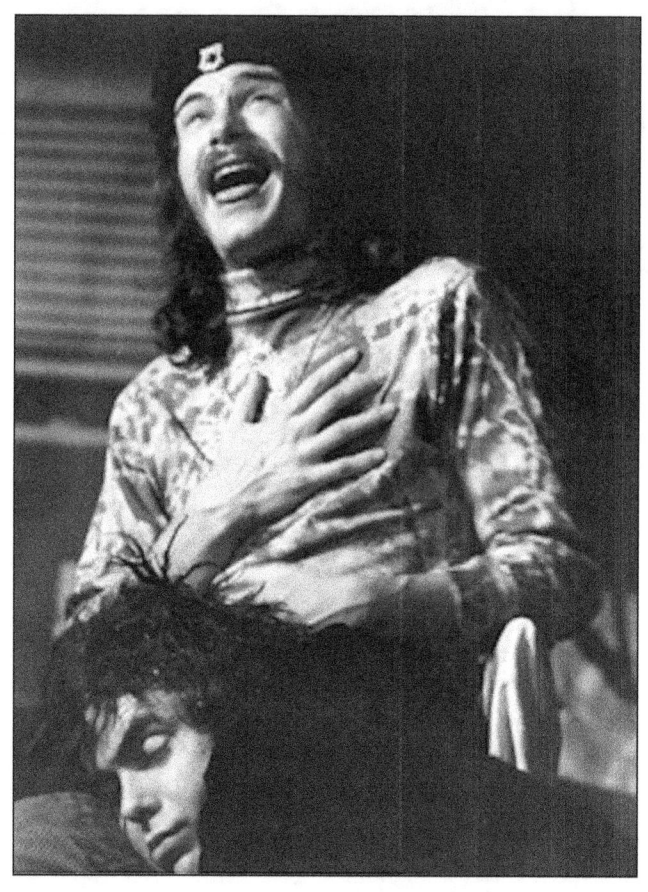

---

**344** Original, *pizza di malafunghi*.

**CONDE:** Come! Hear my feeble croak.
Lift thy doublet, boy. Bend over!
You are not an orphan foundling
As you think, but the one and only son
and true and rightful Heir
to the vast and weighty Fortune
of the King of Arrrrghhh . . .

### *[HE DIES]*

**EDMUNDO:** The King of Arrrrrghhh! I know not a
King of Arrrrgh! I've heard the Duke of Ergh!
[SINGING] Duke, duke, duke of Ergh Ergh Ergh.
Is't him of whom ye speak? What ho?
Art deaf to my entreaties? Nay dead!

*[EDMUNDO DUO appears from behind the arrassio.]*

**ED DUO:** Oh, piteous time! The Count is dead!
I'll bear these tidings to the Queen — in bed!

*[HE DISAPPEARS.]*

**EDMUNDO:** Dead as a donut,[345] this Holey man![346]
Oh, sneaky Death, to nip him like a glass of Bud![347]
How flat, Scruggs and unpotable seem
To me all the ails of this world! He's dead!
Oh, mercenary destiny that marbles up

---

[345] Original, *Morto comme la pizza.*

[346] This soliloquy exists in a burlesque version performed by Irish comedian Junius O'Brien on Edison cylinder MSGV009. Whether he was drunk, ad libbing or delivering a scripted monologue is not known.

    EDMUND: Oh, sneaky Death! To nip me like a glass of Bud! How flat, Scruggs and unpotable seem to me all the ales of this world! I'll bear no more! Bring on the Bear Whiz Beer and whiz both bear and bier and body off! He was a gentle man, an Uncle to the world. The little children loved him, and thus were trained to run between his legs. How fit that he should die outdoors, for oft I saw him walk unwrapp'd 'cross forest lawns. He'd talk to the trees — but they'd not listen to him. He talked to the birds — their awful offal dropping on his shoulders. And from the riches of his treasured chest, he'd shower us with gold! Some died with crushed head, like wealthy men. Like him. Like he. He's dead!

[347] Original, *tasso di vino di aqua.*

The sweetened tooth of Time with black disguise.
I'll fill my bucket silly with revenge,
'Till blood shall douche the anger from mine eyes.

*[ENTER IL CARDINALE]*

**CARD:** Nephew!

**EDMUNDO:** Gazundtheit!

**CARD:** Your couplet runneth over.
Come. In this our hour of mutual greed,
Let's share an urn of churning Burgundy![348]

**EDMUNDO:** I'll drink to that!

**CARD** [*ASIDE*]: He'll drink to anything!
And so my gruesome plan is clear, and now,
I'll do't.
And with Dame Exposition as my Muse
I'll 'splain it thus:
This foundling cur was known to be my brother's
Favourite, and so is bound to find some favor
In his will. So thus, to flavor my good fortune,
I'll pack him off to Heaven's army
By this poisoned draft.
***[HE POISONS THE WINE]***
There to be my bested brother's keeper,
So thus to keep the bastard's best myself!
How keen!
And yet I speak so fast I know not what I mean!
Eddie, my love! Here's drink for you!

**EDMUNDO:** And drink for you!

*[CROSSING ARMS, THEY DRINK FROM THEIR OWN GOBLETS]*

**CARD:** It won't be long. E'en now, the venom's
Rushing to his brain. Hic! Hoc!

---

[348] Original, *tasso di chianti Vesuviano*.

                    Death's knocking
                    At his door, and yet he smiles.

EDMUNDO:        Ha ha!

CARD:           He'll drop, like a stone!³⁴⁹

*[THE BISHOP FALLS AND DIES]*

EDMUNDO:        He's no fun, he fell right over!
                What, Nuncle? Drunk again? Dead drunk!
                Nay — dead! Yet — drunk!
                Oh, double death that takes two Nuncles
                In one day. Where are their smiles?
                Their curd'ling mirth?
                They've left me groatless here
                To seek the sacred secret of my secret birth.
                I'd better take some speed,
                And beat the Queen to Perth.

*[ENTER ED ED, DISGUISED AS COLOMBINA]*

---

**349** Seized by an excess of iambs, Edmundo Duo was once recorded saying:
　　"Come Reno's swift-wing'd justice cart
　　　To catch this falling star.

ED DUO: No, no, you don't!

EDMUNDO: Quelle jolie surprise![350] Cousine Marie! I've saved this little pecker here for thee!

ED DUO: Non! Non! Oui oui! I'm not!

EDMUNDO: What what?

ED DUO: Unbeknownst to you, I am your illegitimate twin Brother — Edmund Edmund!

EDMUNDO: But, Marie! Then never can we married be!

ED DUO: And you shall ne'er recieve my father's fortune!

EDMUNDO: Why should I take a woman's word for that?

ED DUO: 'Nough said! En garde, you swine!

EDMUNDO: I'll guard my swine 'til death do part us both! Have at you!

ED DUO: Gazuntheit!

*[THEY FIGHT AND EDMUNDO DUO IS KILLED]*

EDMUNDO: Suffering St. Succotash![351]
So passes into History,
This holy, homely lass!
She's dead and gone, and yet she acts!

*[EDMUNDO DUO dies an elaborate and unconvincing death. IL CONDE rises from his chair.]*

CONDE: Well fought, my son!

---

Lo, Death's moth-winged Humvee-stretch arrives.
His life is o'er. He'll dropeth like a Sharon Stone."

[350] A curious remnant of the Marivaux version of the play, a controversial work written with the visiting *commedia del'arte* troup.

[351] St. Succotach of Slobovia was martyred by cornholing in 1232.

**EDMUNDO:** My Nuncle's ghost!

**CONDE:** Not your Nuncle, but your Dad!

**EDMUNDO:** My Father's ghost?

**CONDE:** Not a ghost, neither.

**EDMUNDO:** Not my Father?

**CONDE:** Yes, my son.

**EDMUNDO:** I am your son?

**CONDE:** No, no! I am your Father! And I have proof!
Read what is writ upon your dagger's dirk,
The twin to mine.

EDMUNDO: This plastic toy?[352] 'Twas given me at birth.

CONDE: The very same.

EDMUNDO: [*Reads*] "I am he of who he speaks."
That's proof enough for me!

CONDE: And me!

**EDMUNDO DUO and CARDINALE:** And me![353]

CONDE: We are agreed! And so we seal our
Secret kinship with a kiss.

EDMUNDO: Son![354]

CONDE: Father!

*[EMBRACING, THEY RUN UPON ONE ANOTHER'S BLADES]*

CONDE: Alas! I am but hurt!

EDMUNDO: Me too!

ED DUO: There's nothing more to say.

TUTTI: And no one's left to write an ending
To this nawful play.

## [ALL DYE]

### *Il commedio e finito*

---

[352] FT made considerable use of various cheap plastic daggers in their stage performances. *Commedia* authenticity would require the use of elongated "Cyranoses" The line would properly read, "This bloody nose?"

[353] At this point, frightened by the voices of the "dead men," the *commedia* actors would have pulled their dirks and a mock battle would have ensued. Thus the comically "accidental" deaths.

[354] This exclamation point is spurious. ED is saying "*figlio?*" as a question and CONDE replies "*Papa!*" The notion that they confuse their relationships can only be due to exhaustion.

**BISHOP:**
*"How liked you the field pie, Brother?
'Twas of my own making."*

# ADDITIONAL DIALOGUE
## "ACT V" [SEE NOTE SOMEWHERE]

*A GARDEN. ENTER THE COUNT AND NUNCLE BISHOP, ATTENDED BY FRIAR BEEPO.*

**COUNT:** What a wonderful supper!

**BISHOP:** How liked you the field pie, brother?
'Twas of mine own making.

**COUNT:** I liked it only passing well, and so I passed it by,
dear brother. Methought it bore your seal.

**BISHOP:** (*ASIDE*) The bore! That poison pie was sealed and stamped, yet he wouid like it not. And so my stamp is cancelled thus, post-haste, by him — this first-class mail'd man, I mean. And yet, I speak so fast, I know not what I mean.

*THE COUNT SEATS HIMSELF*

**COUNT:** Nor I. Nor all us here. And so, good brother
Bishop, here we sit.

**BISHOP:** Not I.

**COUNT:** Not us, but we — who've stuffed our gullet to the sticking point and signed the treaty with the cows. Our virgin niece is padlocked for the Spanish throne. Faire Normandie is brought to task.

**BISHOP:** And tax! (*ASIDE*) 'Zguts I care! For how am I to turn a dandy leg at court, unless a dandy legacy is turned to me, from him!

**COUNT:** But alas, hairless Brother —

| | |
|---|---|
| **BISHOP:** | Hairless, yes, but heirless too! |
| **COUNT:** | I grow aweary of affairs of state. I fear me that my fatal hour grows neigh. The residue of changing times doth clot my heart. And still no word from my nephew, Edmund? |
| **BISHOP:** | Your witless nephew nightly wassails with the extras and wrestles with your sometime niece. Would you make an heir of one who puts on airs, and takes the air, and gives you nothing, brother mine, but air? (ASIDE) He errs, by Gemini! An errant air-sign and a Jew! |
| **COUNT:** | Adieu? |
| **BISHOP:** | A Jew! |
| **COUNT:** | Goodbye! Farewell! Begone! |
| **BISHOP:** | (ASIDE) I have but begun to begone![355] (HE EXITS) |
| **COUNT:** | I like him better not at all. But how my feverish thoughts do fly upon his hair-line. |

[355] See the excruciatingly long exit of Mole. Here, the Bishop sambas indolently to the wings.

"What does this mean? What dare I do?"
Wiggan Cuppe as "Eddie"
1974 Welcome Vets! Roaring Twenties Revue

# "THE CLOISTER SCENE"

From Ziegfeld's 1928 Production "Shakespeare's Follies"
Starring Eddie Cantor as "Eddie"
and soprano Kitty Carlysle as "Marie"
(Music by Rothman & Klein)

SCENE: *A cloister in the Castle Pflegm. A group of NUNS passes through, barely wrapped in Erte-designed towels, on their way to the steam baths. Enter EDDIE, reading a book upside down.*

> EDDIE (SINGS)
> What does this mean? What dare I do?
> I'm but a man — and yet — a boy!
> Not yet a man. Yet, not a boy neither!
> I am like a little boy,
> Speaking like a man,
> Besuited in tight tights
> That squeeze upon the parts
> That make-ith me forget that
> I'm a little boy!
> What am I?

*MARIE ENTERS IN ERTE'S SWAMP-LIKE TRANSPARENT COCKTAIL GOWN AND EGRET-FEATHER WIG*

> MARIE
> My lord . . .

> EDDIE
> My lord! So this is what I am!

> MARIE
> Art thou wounded?

> EDDIE
> Winded yes, wounded no.
> Wound, yes! And about to be unwound,
> I'll warrant thee!

MARIE
My lord, you're wobbling like a nightingale.

EDDIE
Then give me a limb that I may perch on it.

MARIE
Am I a tree, my lord?

EDDIE
Would that thou wast, that I might fell thee with my love and strip thee of thy virgin bark.

MARIE
Speak thou of dogs, my lord?

EDDIE
No. [ASIDE] Woof!

MARIE
Then I shall sing a *chanson populaire*.

(SINGS) O happy Death,
That chalks the cheeks of rosy Ned
And nips the budding buds of
Bubbling Pud!
'Tis Death! O, happy, happy Death!
O ha-ha-ha-ha-ha-happy
Happy, happy, happy Death!

EDDIE
I hate those French songs.

MARIE
Was I speaking French, my lord?

EDDIE
No, no.
(DRAWING HIS DAGGER DISTRACTEDLY)
Had I half a mind . . .

MARIE
But you have, my lord.

EDDIE
I'd stick this family heirloom where it belongs.

MARIE
Not here? My lord!

EDDIE
(SINGS) There's nothing here for me, save you.
By God!
I'll cut the soles from off my shoes.
We'll walk in trees with common folk
And play upon the flute!
Wouldst play upon my flute, Marie?

MARIE
Oh, Ned!

EDDIE
My sweet Marie!

MARIE
So let's to bed!

EDDIE
Whoopee!

**They exit. Curtain.**

# "SWEET MARIE'S MAD SCENE"
## FROM
# "THE SUFFRAGETTE'S SHAKESPEARE"

This rare and beautiful publication (*My Own Rosebud Press*, Boston 1912) includes several additional scenes for Marie that seem to have been written by the generated Mrs. Syddons for her all-girl production (U.S. Tour 1909-1910) of "Anythynge You Want To" and "Double Falsehood." Marie was played by the lovely Blanche Brin, who later entered a Zen nunnery. Ziegfeld himself glorified the clown, Pestio, who, in Syddon's production, was given to speak-singing short introductions to many scenes in a proto-Brechtian style. They soon became a hallmark of the Follies. The following lines are included here to provide a useful alternative to tiresome audition monologues by Juliet and Lady McBeth.

*MARIE enters singing with an armload of fresh vegetables.*

> [Reprise of "Oh, Happy Death!]
> Here's brouhaha for you . . . and Columbine -
> BANG-BANG! — that's for remembrance!
> Army beans and Navy beans!
> More soya beans — there's profit in't and protein too.
> Here's Rose o' the Plague and Violins d'amour.
> Here's Pestilence made Art and sold like poultry
> I' the Common Square . . .
> He call'd me but a Midge. I a Midge and he a Horse.
> Thou'rt small as a Midge, whil'st I, saith he,
> Built more like a horse-fly do seem to drive you mad!
> O Midge! O Midge!
> Don't go mad, don't be sad!
> Don't fly apart like a little teapot!
> [Sings] Here is my Handel — Hal'o'loolia! Hal'o'loolia!
> Here are my sprouts . . .
> Tip me over and float me out . . . Alas!
> All the sheiks of Araby could not clean these sheets!

**MARIE exits, drowning**

*Channel 6 investigative reporters Harold Hiphugger (l) and Ray Hamberger (r) broadcasting from the Pflegmish borderlands during the "Freedom From Pflem!" marches of 1980.*

# PROGRAM NOTES FOR THE 1980 PFLEGMISH NATIONAL PUBLIC RADIO BROADCAST

*These notes were read live by the internationally distinguished radio and film actor Ben Wright under difficult circumstances off State Motorway A2 at the Iron Curtain Exit.*

**HOST:** I'm standing here on the border of the small European principality of Pflegm, divided during the Second Great War by bitter political strife into the Communist People's Republic of Plaap Pflegm (or COMPLOP) and the Democratic Oligarchy of Hoch Pflegm — a fabulous, glowing casino and glittering safety deposit box for the international jet set. Here, on this very spot . . .

*Here, the Host was nearly struck by a Bulgarian goods van.*

Ah, well — anyway, very near that very spot, loomed the ancient battlements of Castle Pflegm, within which was set the rousing and terrible Elizabethan popular classic favorite (often attributed to Shakespeare) "Anythynge You Want To." Now, 400 years ago, this modern urban motorway and beautiful Pflegmland State Lottery Building were gone — or, rather, were not here yet, and in their place were courage, thirst for power and a primitive open sewer system, running to the sea. Against this muted background our author wrote this play. Perhaps he, like so many others like him, was similar to the members of companies of itinerant performers, drawn to the city by plague, prostitution and, or, penury. Indeed, one could well imagine the Prologue to this play being spoken upon the spot where I now stand . . .

*Here, the Host narrowly avoided collision with a taxi.*

Sorry! Well, perhaps both of us, and you too, would feel more comfortable over here, with out backs against this ancient, er, modern billboard. And if we cock an ear, can we not hear the music of an ancient horn . . . ?

*Here, the Host beats a hasty retreat. At the first Interval, the Host returned to chat with members of the theatre audience attending this premier Royal Broadcast.*

**HOST:** We'll be back to the Pflegmland National Radio Theatre production of "Anythyng You Want To" in just a moment. This interval finds us in the charming and well-lit Commissary of Raadio Pflegm's beautiful Diffusion House, which was, interestingly enough, a vast undersea mooring-pen for submarines during the later days of the Occupation in the Last Great War. So, let's just push ahead in line, and speak to a few of the wealthy dignitaries and rich artistes here today . . . Why, hello — here's Randy Walleroo, rising young Aboriginal film star, appearing in our production as the Corpse of Ned in Act 2, Scene 4. Well, Randy . . .

**RANDY:** Yeah, whot d'yer wont?

**HOST:** What do you think of the play so far?

**RANDY:** Well, mate, they didn't put a radio in me rent-a-car, naow did they? So I really don' know, naow do I? Do I?

**HOST:** Thank you, Randy Wallaroo. Oh! Here is the Queen! What are you having for lunch today, your Majesty?

**QUEEN:** We're having the jello-mold, the Waldorf salad, the Belgian endive salad, the blanc-mange, and — I think — the turkey roll.

**HOST:** We're most honored to have you here for the production, your Majesty.

**QUEEN:** We're leaving directly after lunch.

**HOST:** Well, thank you, m'am. And here, at the front of the line . . .

**ESCROW** . . . 'Ow much is that in pounds? I mean, I haven't got any of your funny wog money. Look — 'ere's everything in me pocket, love, just taike it out of 'ere. Not the cocaine, dear. Give it back, now — give it back! That's a good girl . . .

| | |
|---|---|
| **HOST:** | Excuse me, Derrick. This is Derrick Escrow, the distinguished director of today's play. Derrick, are you satisfied that everything's on schedule so far? |
| **ESCROW:** | Yeah, well — we're gonna shoot the other Berkeley credit card commercial tomorrow, right after the bowl o' Froot-Loops number for the Japos in the a.m. |
| **HOST:** | No, Derrick. The broadcast. The play. |
| **ESCROW:** | Oh, yeah, that thing. Yeah, well, that's alright. I'm satisfied with the lights, the set and the costumes. |
| **HOST:** | Costumes? But it's a radio piece, isn't it? |
| **ESCROW:** | Yeah, well, I suppose it is. But it's all in the authenticity, ain't it? I mean — authenticity, that' the thing today. Yanks in leading roles, the authentic rustle of yer 16th century drag, yer authentic 'oofbeats of a thousand 'orses — and yer bagpipers, yer stone walls, the moat we built. And for that, we had to hire on an authentic Commy crew on top of the regular crew. Then we go into a triple-crew situation on the weekends, when they bring in the flamin' UN to arbitrate! I mean, we wouldn't be 'ere if it weren't authentic, now would we then? You bet we wouldn't be! |
| **HOST:** | Thank you, Derrick. We all think it's going along very well. |
| **ESCROW:** | Right! Well, for you, fine! For me, I've got to rewrite the flippin' third act! Where's me food . . . ? |
| **HOST:** | And now, let's return for Act Two of "Anythynge You Want To" . . . |

*Return they did for the justly famous Coronation and Graveyard Picnic Scenes. At the second interval, the Host took a brief pre-produced audio tour of the then politically, culturally and, with a Wall, divided country. He began in the Salle de Luxe of Hotel Caastle Pflegm.*

| | |
|---|---|
| **HOST:** | We'll return in a moment to the exciting third and final act of "Anythynge You Want To," produced in Radio Pflegm's Diffusion House, with an international cast, and the generous support and co-operation provided by The Warm Shoe Fund, |

the COMPLOP People's Electricultural Exchange Secretariat and the Social Image Ministry of FlemNuke Ltd. It's said that Shakespeare never visited Pflegm. Well, it's also said that Shakespeare never wrote this play. But if he had, and many believe that he could have done, he would have stayed where our production is presently quartered, in the partitioned luxury of Caastle Pflegm. Here, in the Free World Wing, celebrities and NATO generals alike bump and gamble the night away, whilst just across this chamber — just beyond that simple strand of hot, charged wire — is the Red Wing, where COMPLOP party functionaries and ranks of stern-faced filing clerks shuffle papers from midnight to dawn, planning, one must suppose, for the day to come. What force fuses them together? Power!

*Briefly, we hear the sound of many typewriters and a dance band from the opposite sides of Pflegm.*

**HOST:** For, outside that gorgeous bank of leaded renaissance windows, one can easily see, whenever the protective shutters are raised, the imposing nuclear condensing tower, christened Friendship Stack, which dominates the atomic installation operated by the two governments. Far from being a mutually insane, last-ditch adventure in cynical opportunism, in fact, Friendship Stack has proven to be a boon to both light industry and heavy tourism in this otherwise chronically depressed land. And, the almost daily emergencies serve to bring these divided peoples closer together in a country where the phrase "nuclear family" has a particularly emotional significance.

Well, as Shakespeare may or may not have said, in a line nearly excised from this production, for reasons of time:

> "When warring brothers raise their stakes,
> Lest Civil War be fought,
> 'Tis better they lay down their hands
> And divvy up the pot."

Wise words. Now, Act Three of "Anythynge You Want To."

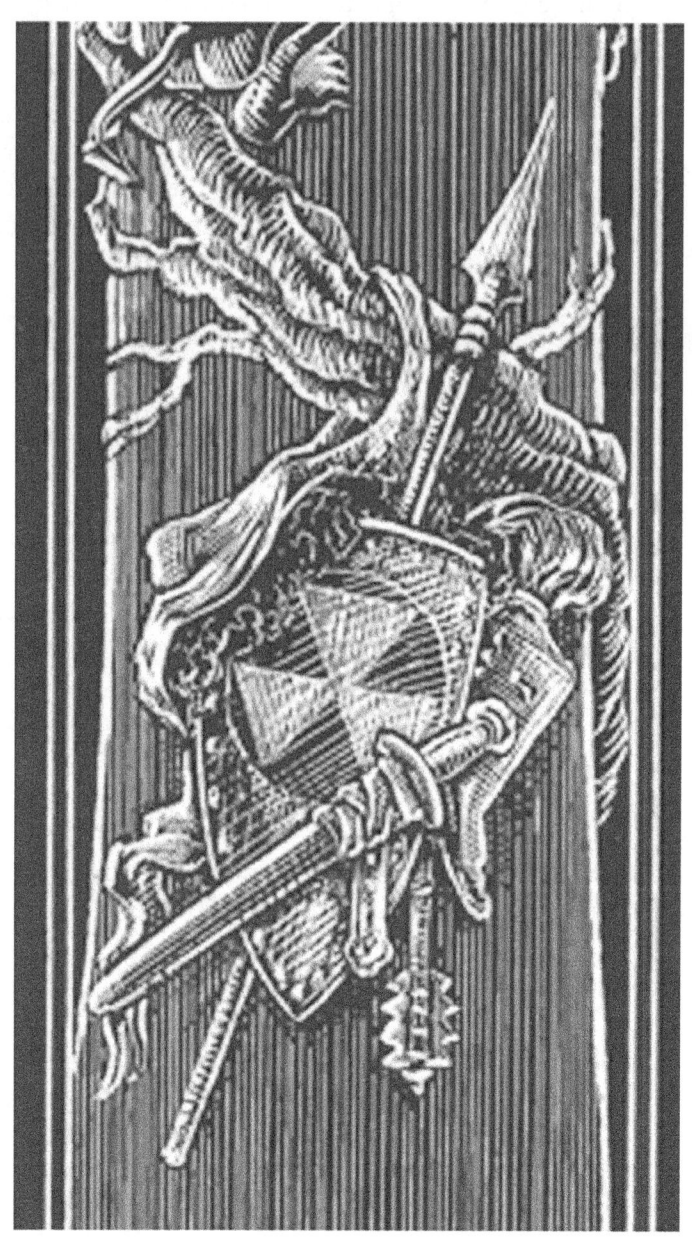

# DRAMATURGICAL ANALYSIS OF "ANYTHYNGE YOU WANT TO"

GENTS,

I've thought this over and looked at the order of the scenes in several different ways. The problem is, and let's get this out at the start, *Edmund* disappears from the play in Act III in almost any other configuration. If we include the new material, in bold below, in our 1995 performances, I think the following is the best way to proceed.

Our Act One would contain the following three scenes, with some dialogue restored in Scenes 1 and 3:

    SCENE ONE – A SHIP AT SEA
    Boson — DO
    Sailors — PA, PB, PP
    Stormendrain — PP
    Happenstance — PB
    Edmund Edmund — PA

    INTERACTIVE CHOICES:
(A) As a Chinese Opera, (B) Gilbert & Sullivan, (C) On The Town

    SCENE TWO – THE BLASTED HEATH
    Cooks — PA, PP
    Count — DO
    Bishop — PB

    INTERACTIVE CHOICES:
(A) Welles' Voodoo Version, (B) Julia Childs' Kitchen, (C) Welles Film Macbeth

### SCENE THREE – RAMPARTS OF CASTLE PFLEGM
Pete — PB
Andrew — PA
Ghost — DO
Edmund — PP

"Exactly as performed in Shakespeare's Globe Theatre since 1605."

That's easy enough. Now for the all-new Act Two. The movement toward the water works well, and we now need to know that Edmund Edmund is alive and on the trail of the Sacred Pot.

### SCENE FOUR – THE SEASHORE
Flounder — DO
Edmund Edmund — PA

This ought to be really Surreal. Pete and Phil could play The Walrus and The Carpenter.

### SCENE FIVE – BISHOP'S CHAMBER
Bishop — PB

The soliloquy only, re-establishing the Bishop's Atomic Powered mission. Could we have a flaming cauldron or something electric from "Frankenstein?"

### SCENE SIX – COUNT'S CLOSET
Count — DO
Cardentte — PP
Fangboner — PA
Pestio — PB

The first two pages only. This is all about clothes.

### SCENE SEVEN – THRONE ROOM
Fangboner — PA
Steward — PP
Count — DO
Fairfax — PB
Mulholland — PP

Burbank — PA
Edmund Edmund — PA
Bishop — PB

Count is crowned off-stage between scenes. Now, the movie production scene edited and simplified. Edmund Edmund does the cigar business which is from the previous scene.

### SCENE EIGHT — THE BATTLE GROUND
Grapeshot — PB
Muzzle — PP
Edmund Edmund — PA
Marinara — DO

Bodies everywhere. World War One. Smoke pots.

And now, our Act Three. Additional dialogue (by Rick Shakespeare) makes the transition to *Il Conde di Monte Cristo*. Changing one word ("plague") to ("war") will give the impression the battle has created this increased digging.

### SCENE NINE — GRAVEYARD
Hole — PA
Mole — DO
Edmund — PP
Bishop — PB
Edmund Edmund — PA

Funny props and traditional "Hamlet" costumes. (See Olivier)

### SCENE TEN — "WAITING ON THE COUNT OF MONTE CRISTO..."
Conde — DO
Cardinale — PB
Edmundo — PP
Edmundo Duo — PA

We should do this with false noses, wigs and "commedia" costumes.

Obviously, dear friends, we can do Prologue/Act One (17 pp) and Act Three (11 pp) and not Act Two (13 pp) as we have been doing, especially for the Interactive Hoo-Ha.

In the 43 page version I will be giving you tomorrow, I have linked the recorded play with The Count by inserting few likeable lines from the last scene, adding some new dialogue lines here and there, and hoping the audience will follow along. I'm hopeful that the arc of the story, as it involves each of our main characters, will be complete enough to read "five act Elizabethan play."

I see Rick defending the integrity of his ancestor's work and Escrow willing to compromise it for commercial reward. Peter, I think, could project himself as the Renaissance Man Rick S. by acting, arguing and "producing" it all. He has to tell the story of the underwater discovery, etc.

Phil A should portray Jan Groot, our Interactive Guide.

If PP as Director Escrow differs with Producer Shakespeare over interpretation, and with Actor Austin over improv vs. rehearsal, DO should be the Critic/Dramaturge on the panel (as PP suggests) and no one agrees with him on anything. A Marxist? A Sexist?

I think the story of the origin of the play that PP lays out as Director Escrow can be bitterly contested by Rick S, who says he found the drowned MS off Bermuda, by the Critic who sees the whole play as being about sex, clothes and all anarchy to the monarchy! And by the Actor who just sees it all as "Text, man."

As for structure, I like the play bursting out of the panel, using the disguised-as-Marie challenge of Ed Ed as the point to Enter The Text and provoke a beat of comic swordplay. My Critic character can be killed immediately, and the Actor chases PP as Escrow off the stage. Rick S. can, after the fight is quieted, introduce the actors by way of the Prologue — and PP and DO can effect changes off and reappear as the appropriate characters.

In an even shorter version, the audience can be give "choices" (by Jan Groot?) as to the interpretation of Scenes 1 and 2 (or even the order they are done in) but we are required by the Globe Trust to do Scene 3 as it Always Has Been Done.

PB then bumps the Text forward to Scene 5, the Bishop's soliloquy. DO as Swaggar bumps the Text forward to Scene 9, the Graveyard, a course acting fave. Jan Groot then clicks us on to the Commedia original Text.

See ya tomorrow night!

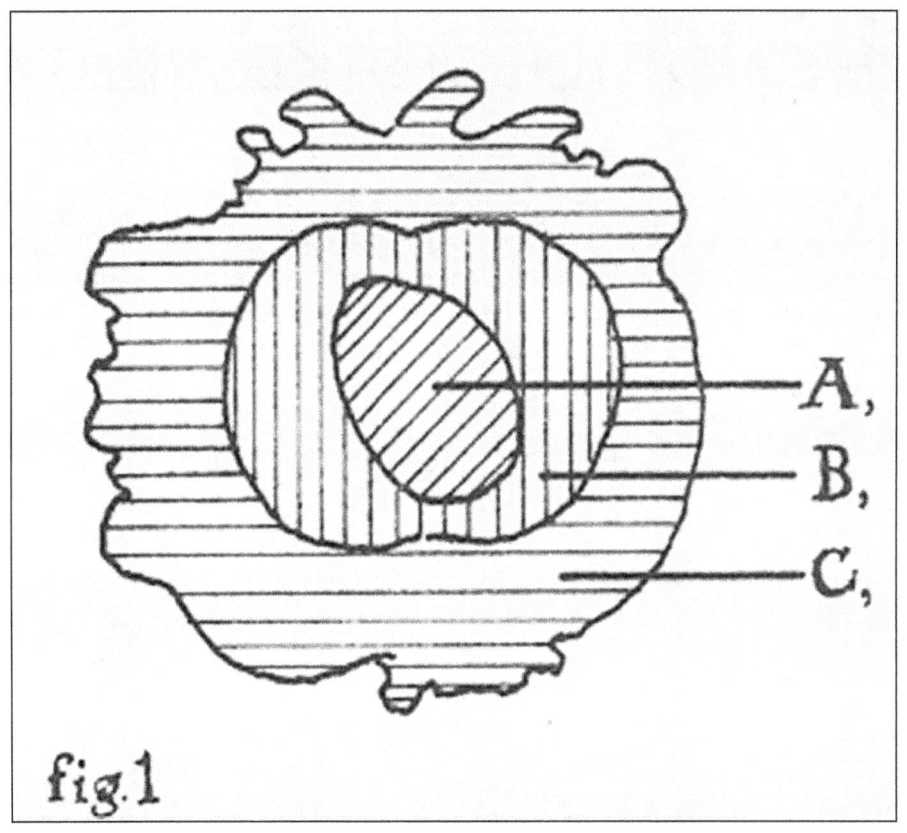

### GLOBE SALAD
*This vehicle of theatrical criticism consisted of a rotten plover's egg, A, ensconced in an overly ripe tomato, B, itself encased in a hideously bloated cabbage, C. Audiences at the Globe Theatre would hurl these wicked devices at offending actors or throw them at the poor upon leaving the theatre in order to improve their sense of charity and aim. This dish has since become a favorite amongst insane British vegetarians.*
*Illustration by Bruce Litz for Chef Croquette's "Projectile Cookery."*

# "THE EDIBLE SHAKESPEARE"

In *ibid* after *ibid*, the annotators of *Anythynge You Want To* have referenced the 1935 cookbook *The Edible Shakespeare* by Chef (and food scholar) Gianbatista Croquette.[356] These unusual recipes have been entertainingly demonstrated by the Chef's son, "Dr. Gravy" on his Public Television Series, "Anything You Want To Eat."[357] We offer a selection of them here, for those food enthusiasts who wish to eat appropriately while enjoying the play.

HONEYMOON PICNIC FOR TWO
(see note, Act III, sc. 2)

First, take a nice, clean Box, line it with checkered flags and put a soft pillow inside. Now, you buy

> 2 dozen "Love-Crossed Clams" (*labium rock*.)
> 2 English Head Bangers (or Pflegmish Blootwurst)
> 2 16-oz bottles of Old Sod Stout Bitter Ale
> 1/2 dozen nice, plump Sweet Buns
> 1 stick of Fresh Cream Brando Farm Butter
> 1/2 pound assorted Cold Cuts (Well-Mounded)
>> Honey Ham
>> Pflegmish Baloney
>> Turkey Loaf
>> Breasts, etc.

Pack them up nice and tight to keep them warm and prepare:

---

[356] Ladies' Housekeeping Journal Co., Milwaukee 1935, Thos. Cooke & Sons, Lerndon, 1934, reprinted by Cool Old Stuff Press, Cambridge, 1978, and again by Forgotten Books, Berkeley, 2002.

[357] Unlike his father, whose Chef's career included Packard House, Snob Hill Hotel, The Astor-Styvesant and The Melody Room, and who was awarded the Grande Cordon Pflegmoise (first given in 1518 by King Enery) by the *Ecole National des morceau d'eaux*, "Gravy" went directly from hot-plate to video after he opened Castratti's — a bar serving signature small dishes based on themes from writers and artists. His own best-selling cooking guide, *Everything You Want To Eat is Wrong* has recently been joined by *Ready-Made Meals*, based on works by Marcel Duchamp, featuring "infrathin" dining ideas and suggestions like "Use a Rembrandt as a toaster oven."

### JELLIE ROLE A LA FRANCOISE:

Take one big bowl of dough, if you can get it. Spread it and roll it around. Lay it out long and thick. Coat, like a tongue, with Mousse Framboise, *petit choux* and marinate in *eau de vie Bohemienne*. Warm it in your oven until mature. Place the Jellie Role and Picnic Clams into the Box, and find a secluded place — graveyards are best — and let Come What May!

### DEVILS BAR-B-QUE
(see note, Act I, sc. ii)

Assemble a gutted razor-back hog (about 40 lbs) and stuff with Razor Clams in their shells, then roast. Serve with Chicken Fried Cuttlefish, Hot Whelp Soup, Countrywide Deep Fried Potatoes with Cornholes and Sides of Holy-peño Pepper Shots

Peckers Up Ale, Southern Dis-Comfort and Moldy's Old Rye

### TYPICAL ENGLISH OATMEAL BREAKFAST
(see note, Act I, sc. ii)

Prepare a thick Scotch gruel of peat, a mess of sheep's pottage, and onyx eggs (blackened and highly polished before serving). Put on a plate with Melted Toast, Minishrooms in Strange Gravy and Sweet Baked Beans.

### EASTER TREFOIL CAKES
(see note Act II, sc. i)

The cakes: use groat flour, holy water, simple sugar, and blue, yellow and red food coloring; bake and stuff with Blootwurst (imported from Pflegm, you can still get it at Zygots, Trader Hans and Holey Foods).

The cakes are deep-frozen first and then warmed in a slow oven (just like Sts. Grid, Goofus and Walto, the patron trinity of animators).

Best served with a block of frozen AquaVit and Jam.

## STUFFED CODPIECE IN THE TUDOR MANNER
(see note, Act III, sc. i)

As will be remembered, Tudor costuming featured a comic take on the Male Member with one Enery trying to out-do another by padding, quilting or otherwise inflating the front of his "slops."

Chef Crockette places Gooey Ducks — a humiliatingly large-necked (or footed) Northwestern clam — in a pleated puff-paste baguette with twin cod cheeks, gets them all hot and bothered and serves them naked on a plate. It's not pretty.

## COOKING FOR ROYALTY

(from "Gravy" Crockette's *Flavorless Foods*, this list of buffet selections appropriate for crowned heads, as served to the Queen at Castle Hoch Pfleghm, 1980):

ED'S WALDORF SALAD — stale walnuts, apples, ale and sugared meat, and
HOTEL SALAD — steamed for two days over hot water
FOWL A LA KING — Creamed Cock Surprise with Soft Noodles, Mystery Greens and/or
TURKEY ROLLS — meatless, hat-shaped and felt-like finishing with
BLANC-MANGE — a sort of jellied pudding-like mange, or
JELLIED MOLD — a jiggly assortment of mold cubes

## "A WONDERFUL SUPPER!"
Since characters in plays are forever entering the stage after having eaten a meal off-stage, Chef suggests three off-stage choices for catering:

## FIELD PIE or PIZZA DI CAVALLO (*Il Conde*)
"Morto comme la pizza" as the saying goes. Lotsa dough, big cheeses, saucy, spicy and no anchovies. A nice piece serves a whole actor.

## GENUINE GYPSY STEW (Act I, sc. ii)
For night rehearsals, "Dr. Gravy" suggests a powerful double-tall soy protein potion with bananas, benzedrene and Spanish fly.

## A BATTLEFIELD PICNIC (Act IV, sc. ii)

Uncle Nudinudo's Hot Sausage (Sour Krauts, knocked their worst) dredged in Orphan's Tears and served on a slab. Good for closing night parties — serves everyone right.

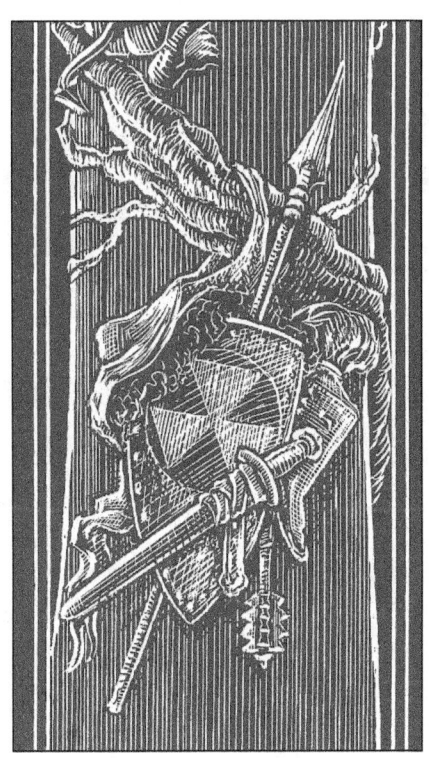

*Leander McVootie as Fullstaffe*

# "SHINANNIGAN!"
## ORSON WELLE'S EXPOSE OF "SHAKESPEARE'S LOST COMEDY"
### Treatment by David Ossman
## THE GREATEST SHENANNIGAN OF THE 16TH CENTURY!

*"Shakespeare never wrote ANYTHYNGE YOU WANT TO, and I never directed it. The whole business was a Fake!"*
*Orson Welle's*

This movie is a vehicle designed expressly for JOHN GOODMAN and THE FIRESIGN THEATRE, plus celebrity and comedy Guest Stars.

The late ORSON WELLE'S (played by John Goodman) has left behind a few last scraps of unreleased film. They have been cobbled together with bits of Welle's personal recollections by Australian MTV and commercial director Derrick Escrow. What Escrow finally makes is an "F is for Fake" meets "Hard Copy" sort of expose, in which the Great Welle's proves that Shakespeare probably never wrote his greatest play, *Anythyne You Want To*, and also recounts the soundstage shenanigans that plagued his own long-unfinished film production of the play.

**FADE IN:**

GOODMAN'S Welle's is seen in that flattering medium shot, complete with wine glass, pipe, general girth, and raised eyebrow, so beloved by directors Henry Jaglom, Peter Bogdanovitch and Paul Masson. Welle's is as genial as Santa Claus, but underneath cynical and self-myth-making.

Welle's narrates us through the first of several Scenes from History — Welle's-ian dramatizations of the Diary and Letters of Pflegmish merchant seaman JAN GROOT (played by Phil Austin), who luckily witnesses an early Elizabethan stage production of *Anythynge You Want To* while in port in "Lerndon, Egland" in 1605.

Groot sees a jolly band of rascals — YE FYRESYGNE THEATRE (Austin, Bergman, Ossman, Proctor) — captivate an audience of Groundlings, cutting a few purses and kissing a few lasses before launching into the comico-dramatic introduction known as *The Prologue*:

We watch Groot enjoying the show, which he doesn't understand, being Hoch-Pflegmish, and writing his glowing review of it in a letter home to his wife or mother. We witness Ye Fyresygn's dumb-show condensation of the entire play through Groot's eyes. (In fact, Groot is a dumb-show all by himself, and reappears, not surprisingly, at future "right moments" in History.)

Next, we meet Aussie director DERRICK ESCROW (played by Phil Proctor), interviewed (actually, interviewing himself) in some remote and probably exotic location. "It was my duty," he says, "to bring Orson Welle's greatest triumph to the screen, even though it was a disaster from every standpoint. Given the money, I'm sure he would have filmed the first scene as I did."

We see Escrow's postmodern interpretation of the play's *Scene One* — set on shipboard during a fierce hurricane. It's part Chinese Opera, part "Pirates of Penzance," part Light & Magic. Lots of grand but gaudy digital special effects stuff — waves, sea creatures, Gulliver, the Swiss Family Robinson, Jaws, Jurassics. Would look great in a video game. Ends flashily.

Welle's returns to chuckle over the history of his unfinished film — made on old cowboy movie sets at Vasquez Rocks, lip-sinc'ed to pre-recorded dialogue, with absurd rented costumes and phony Scottish accents. He shows us some almost-discarded footage of flubs. The actors are really familiar, and there are lots of under-costumed extras.

Welle's recollections are supported by interview clips from RICK SHAKESPEARE (played by Peter Bergman), William's heir and the original collaborator on Welle's production, who remembers wrestling with both Welle's and the script, but who strongly disagrees with Welle's about interpretation. Rick, who is credited with the discovery at sea of a lost manuscript of the play, especially objects to all the editing and rearranging of the text.

He in fact would have begun the film with *Scene Two* — where the WEIRD COOKS are stirring up a Right-wing-talk-show stew in the machine-made smoke on the backlot heath. We see it in the much-admired black-and-white Welle's version (which looks a lot like The Scottish Play).

Welle's returns to talk about the next great scene he managed to get filmed, about how he was jealous that Larry Olivier had all that money and how he, Orson, had to play "Ghenghis Khan" to finance *Anythynge*, and how he really poured it on for *Scene Three* — in which Edmund sees the Ghost on the Castle Tower.

Not surprisingly, this black-and-white mini-masterpiece looks like Oliver's "Hamlet," but with all the kinks showing through — boom shadows, zippers on armor, extras not paying attention, difficult camera moves not quite achieved. Lots of fog. It has been edited out of fragments filmed in two wildly different locations, so the day-for-night effect varies, as do mustaches and vistas. (It's also obvious that the 1955 actors are the same ones seen previously in 1605 and 1995.)

Returning to the documentary, Escrow bemoans the fact that Welle's never filmed *Scene Four* — the encounter on the seashore of Edmund Edmund and the fishy beachcomber, Flounder. He, Escrow, has made it just as the Master would.

First, Jan Groot is seen in a Dramatized Episode from History, much admiring the stage performance of the "fyshhee who'd walk like a man!"

Then, THE GREAT SHENANNIGAN (George Tirebiter, played by David Ossman) is seen in another Dramatized Episode, illustrating the great gulf of interpretations of the role, with a recreation of Shenanigan's 1905 melodramatic reading of the part when he travelled with Dr. Firesign's Travelling Buffalo Show.

Finally, we cut to the film as directed by Escrow, which stars JOHN GOODMAN and/or STEVE MARTIN in a very "Waiting for Godot"-like space-time condominium on an Existential seashore. The beach setting looks warmer than Pflegmland's dyked North Sea shores, however.

*Scene Five* — the Bishop's famous soliloquy beginning, "Really! My experiments in magnifying power do threat to run awry . . ." Naturally, this was Welle's favorite acting bit — right out of his Voodoo "Moby Faustus." We see Welle's cinema interpretation (a long mime with few spoken words to a voice-over of the soliloquy), in its entirety. It has all the cinematic scope of "Citizen Kane."

We also see Jan Groot watching the original Fyresygn Theatre performance for an impossibly contemporary "Atomic" interpretation. In this one, Flounder makes an unexpected entrance with two crazed monks which drives the Groundlings wild.

In the next documentary sequence, Escrow recalls two other memorable recordings of the Bishop's Speech — the first, which we see in very jerky black and white newsfootage, is of HUEY LONG declaiming a few lines just before he is assassinated by Jan Groot. The second, culled from Ken Burns' epic of Baseball, depicts BABE RUTH quoting from the speech in his immortal "Farewell to Baseball." Both these celebrities are played by Mr. John Goodman.

Escrow then introduces us to his dazzling interpretation of *Scene Six* — in which the Count is dressed for his coronation.

This is a grandiose parody (for a couple of minutes) of the lavish French and English Courts seen in recent historical films. Fussy and elaborate costumes are Escrow's downfall here, what with the wigs falling off and all. It finally erupts in a basketball game that continues, sweeping through mirrored hallways, over-staffed with guards, waiters and serving-people, rippling with the noblemen in their uniforms of jeans, t-shirts and cowboy boots, blue William Morris suits and darkglasses, into the nearly-empty soundstage "throne room."

In *Scene Seven*, the Coronation signals the epic conversion of Phlegmland's economy from feudalism to Film-making. We see this actual movie actually being made, with Escrow (or is it Edmund) on the boom, Rick Shakespeare hobnobbing with GOODMAN, CHASE, ANDERSON, OVITZ, SPIELBERG, etc., and Jan Groot again a passive witness to Our Times, quoting immortal lines from the drama. Filmed in the office tower at Universal. That's right, we buy the company!

[At this point, we see superimposed over the Plegmish movie set is a still of the Washington Monument. The Music sounds like Victory At Sea. Another still — The Grand Canyon. A third — the Goodyear Blimp over Metropolis. The music fades and we see a distinguished figure of authority, perhaps COLIN POWELL or BILL O'RIELLY, either or both played by John Goodman. He is sitting behind a desk in the Dept. of Colored Lights Video Center.

**POWELL (or O'REILLY)**
Hello, this is Orson Welles. Right now we are all participating in a Citizen's Alert. Don't worry about doing anything. Your concern is enough at this stage.

He gets up and goes to an illuminated chart on the wall, and uses a pointer to describe it. The bottom panel on the chart is lit with a flashing green light and says ECO-ALERT. He points to the second panel, which lights up amber and reads CITIZEN'S ALERT.

**POWELL (or WELLES)**
We are here. What does this mean? Certainly nothing, if nothing more happens. However, if anything does, we will all be on NEWS ALERT and thus informed as to where It is and what It means to you — the residents of your area. Be sure and tune to . . .

The third panel lights up red — NEWS ALERT! — He keeps speaking, saying, "The U-Sinc Emergency Laser Netweb Grid at 98.6 for normal reception in Your Area."

However, we actually hear a c&w announcer:
GOOD OL' BOY: KMIX, Owl Radio, all day, all night. The Country-Western Emergency spot on your backyard barbeque dial! Now, back to your battle scene!]

*Scene Eight* encompasses the twin Battle Scenes, which, we learn, neither Welle's nor Escrow had the money to stage properly.

We are shown the available footage, two sixty-second sequences, one of which looks like a Froot Loops TV spot, the other like a black-and-white Berkeley Bankcard commercial. Either or both have Japanese subtitles. One is shown upside down.

For *Scene Nine* — the Graveyard scene — we return with Welle's voice-over to the thrilling days of the Elizabethan era, and see the scene as performed by Ye Fyresygn Theatre, with their absurd costumes (including voluptuous drag for "Marie") and rubber chicken props, going for laffs from the appreciative Groundlings.

When this scene is over, and before the play reaches its climactic scene, Welle's presents his proof. The entire "Shakespeare" opus, he claims, is based on an Old Italian Recipe. As a demonstration, Welle's mounts *Scene Ten* — a *commedia dell'arte* stage production filmed in Technicolor, of the final Shakespearian scene of poison, revenge, swordfighting and general comic mayhem. In it, Welle's plays the porculent "Fullstaffe," interacting as the Fifth Crazee Guy with Ye Olde Fyresygne. The Groundlings really dig it! Huzzah! Cries of "Author!" "Author?"

In the documentary wrap-up, Escrow, Groot, Shenanigan and Rick all make final sound-bite appearances to prove, once and for all, that everything you know about *ANYTHING YOU WANT TO* is wrong!

**FADE TO BLACK**

**RICK SHAKESPEARE**, *Beverly Hills, 2011*

# PHIL AUSTIN'S "ADDITIONAL DIALOGUE BY RICK SHAKESPEARE"

## I

Burial Rock is a slick black shoal that lurks just below the roiling surface of the open Pacific ocean some thirty miles off the Southern California coast. On a stormy day some years ago, a day darkening by the minute, a little boat swung near it, anchored between this hazard and the shattered pinnacles of the uninhabited Bleak Islands.

Twenty foot waves were breaking around the bases of the Bleaks and nervous men worked the dive equipment on the steeply rocking deck. They peered anxiously into the water, hoping against hope that they were not about to run onto the shoal. The sun was about to set and their diver had been down too long and now this squall seemed to be getting worse. The captain of dive boat "Salamander" was worried as well, worried about the fact that his client that day had trained a pistol at him and kept it aimed in his general direction no matter how the little boat rocked. The anchor, it seems, was not to be raised.

The man paying the bills that day — and for some days previous — the man holding the gun was in fact, presumed to be a treasure hunter, someone searching the depths for ancient drowned ships. The Captain didn't know for sure even this much. The hunter was a man in his fifties, perhaps, with an old-fashioned mustache and goatee and not much hair on top, a man who refused to give his name and for that privilege had paid double the usual fees.

Again the captain explained the danger of their position and again the man refused to bring his diver up and head for port. Down there, the day before at last light, the submariner had seen something with a corner to it, square or rectangular and just out of his reach as his air ran out. This day had been spent finding the spot. Oxygen was sapped again. Light was fading. Waves were rising. The radio crackled.

"Siddown, Cap," the hunter growled. "He's got it."

And as if on some motion picture cue, some coincidence only seen in darkened theaters, bubbles suddenly burbled and the diver came up, water pouring off the dome of his steel helmet.

One hundred and eighty feet down, under a shelf cut into Burial Rock, overhung by the stalks of the giant kelp forest in an underwater world as strange as any on this earth, the diver had indeed found something.

Tucked into the embrace of the rotted hull of an ancient ship was the intact box of a Sixteenth Century seaman's trunk and inside it was a literary treasure of measureless value, if you believe the story. The treasure had the name Shakespeare on it, or something quite like it. And the man who found and claimed it had the same name.

This is the way he tells it, and he is the man with the pistol as well as the name. There are different stories, to be sure, and many of them do not match the hunter's version, but he was there, as he likes to say, and he knows what he knows.

## II

The sodden trunk had once belonged to a Dutch sailor named Jan Groot, a man forced into service on an English ship bound for the Virginia colonies, who then fled around the entire continent of South America, possibly with the pirate Drake, to escape servitude or worse in the Croatan Colony. Why he had a players' copy of the obscure work called Anythynge You Want To — an Elizabethan potboiler until then never judged to be among the canon of Shakespearian works, will be addressed later.

Clearly it is the name that is of first importance. The treasure hunter says the name "Wlym. Shekspare" is clearly visible on the first page even after four hundred years of submersion. He says modern science was able to preserve it. He will show no one the evidence, awaiting the publication of his book about the whole affair. He says a lot of things.

His name is William Richard "Rick" Shakespeare and not only is he a treasure hunter who will stop at virtually nothing to get what he wants — a man obviously not to be trifled with — but he is as well a long-time Hollywood film producer and former high-level studio executive and, strange as it may seem, a genuine figure of scholarly regard in a little-known backwater of academia. The study of Elizabethan Minor Authors must inevitably feed at the trough of Shakespearean scholarship, but for a man with the Bard's name itself, the path he took must have seemed even more obvious.

There is the name, after all.

And there must be some sense in the man that others — even those denizens of Babylon itself — will of necessity look down on even a Shakespeare whose best-known films are *Gas Babes of Jupiter* and *She Sure Likes to Do It!* Despite his graduation cum laude from Princeton, his co-producer credit on the much-praised Robert Altman film *Clambake!* (1965) and his odd reputation for scholarship in something approaching the classics, the films for which Rick Shakespeare has been responsible on a day-to-day basis have been set squarely in the lower middle of the popular taste and have been forgotten much as that public has forgotten its last meal.

In other words, there must be something in the man that thirsts for respectability.

"Ricky" Shakespeare grew up in the mountain country between North California and South Oregon commonly called Jeffersonia, a place most notable for an ill-fated attempt at secession from the Union in the Nineteen-Forties. The only son of Filmore and Mistryle Shakespeare was delivered in Dunsmuir above Shasta Lake in the twisty dark canyon of the upper Sacramento where to this day the lonely lumber trains chug up and down the mountain.

Filmore Shakespeare, to this day — and his days are certainly numbered in the low tens — refuses to understand who William Shakespeare is or was and Ricky himself only began to understand the considerable weight of his last name upon enrollment in a drama class at Chico State where, for the first time, it dawned on him what people had been talking about for most of his young life.

He hadn't been much of a farm kid but still he pitched in and tried to help on the family ranch. He was clever enough to gain admittance to a college and became a denizen of the English Department at Humboldt State in the so-called Quad Cities (Yreka, Eureka, Yucaipa and Ukiah) of California, and discovered there that many people, most people in fact, knew of William Shakespeare a good deal more than they did Filmore and Mistryle and Ricky.

He got a degree and then a graduate scholarship to Princeton where his thesis, "Amazynge Anythynge" won him a good deal of attention, if not academic notoriety. He wrote a kind of mystery novel about the death of Christopher Marlowe called *Right in the Eye!* (Grove Press, 1965) which was made into a quickly-forgotten movie *In Your Eye!* (Paramount Pictures 1967) which starred James Coburn and Julie Christie. In it, the budding playwright Marlowe is stabbed by the Bard himself. He found himself drawn to Hollywood and never looked back, until—as he likes to say — he looked back.

## III

He was older, he found, and unfulfilled. He searched around his life and found nothing. He was slim enough and rich enough. He was happily divorced from the former Miss Arizona. He owned a million dollar yacht. He hung out with his friends, men like himself for whom Hollywood had once a penchant and whom it had now forgotten. He played a lot of tennis and one day, like a man fingering his ex-wife's jewelry, casually picked up his old studies in Elizabethan Minor Authors. That's the story he tells. The fact that he had in the meantime acquired a Sixteenth Century manuscript with the name Shakespeare on it under suspicious circumstances is something to which he gives no real notice.

"I had more money than I knew what to do with and I had a brain that hadn't been used in over thirty years. I remembered that brain, I got reacquainted with that brain. And that brain needed a good deal more of a challenge than it was getting in the film business," he says.

He returned to learning and writing with a vengeance, attending classes at USC, beginning a serious, expensive, self-financed and rigorous study of the manuscript found in the drowned trunk, haunting the Huntington Library in Pasadena with its precious collection of Shakespearian folios, and beginning work on what was to become his passion, his legacy, his end. It is called *The Bard's Last Joke: The True Story of Anythynge You Want To and Its Secret Authorship by William Shakespeare.* It has yet to find a publisher.

Is Rick Shakespeare a descendant of our Great Poet? And, if so, has he anything of the Great Poetry residing in him? Even if, as many claim, he is the actual author of "Anythynge You Want To" or has at least emended the version we have today by a series of clever manipulations of truth and scholarship, are those emendations good enough to stand up to his four hundred year-old ancestor?

And then, as if all this were not enough, there is the truly odd coincidence that he looks just like the few pictures we have of William Shakespeare himself. He looks just like Shakespeare, if the bard had dressed in the style of American toughs of the Nineteen-Fifties; black shirts and thin pink ties and snap-brim hats. He sports a kind of jazz version of a Van Dyke mustache and beard, he's bald on top and has a handsome Shakespearean dome, but lately wears his side locks tucked back into an elaborate ducktail.

When you meet him, two questions arise. The first is as to the authenticity of the story of Jan Groot and his passage to Virginia and then California. The second is as to the authenticity of the manuscript attributed to William Shakespeare. An answer to either of these questions hangs on whether you believe anything at all of what Rick Shakespeare is more than happy to tell you.

He works out of his home, actually out of a second story above the five-stall garage complex set in back of his eighteen thousand square-foot Faux Spanish mansion in the hills of Beverly. At one time he employed a scholar of lesser-known Elizabethan literature as his assistant and collaborator, but let her go under troubled circumstances. He says now he works alone. His mansion can be seen from afar.

Once in his office there is nothing visible of the Sixteenth Century. Computers on shining bare granite slabs are the only appurtenances. There is expensive Art on the walls. He was at one time the head of a major Hollywood studio, but the only memento of those days is a photograph of him wrestling playfully with the actor Charles Bronson. He can be quite charming when he wants to.

"You tell me," he said, playfully. "What is 'Anythynge You Want To'? How would you describe it? Who wrote it, for instance?"

"No one wrote it," I told him. "It's too bad to have been written. The best guess is that it was largely made up by the actors and then written down by people in the audience in order to prove to others that something so bad could actually exist. It wasn't written by Shakespeare, if that's what you're thinking."

"It's exactly what I'm thinking." He stared at me. "Can you imagine what it is then worth?"

"I've thought about it," I said. "But it isn't by Shakespeare."

"Yes. It is."

"William Shakespeare?"

"I didn't write it, so what other Shakespeare is there?"

He was dead serious. "For the first time," he said. "there's proof. And the mice are going to beat a path to my mousetrap."

## IV

The history of Walter Raleigh in the New World revolves around the settlement often called the Lost Colony, on Croatan Island in what is now the state of North Carolina. To connect "Anythynge You Want To" with that enterprise is half of Rick Shakespeare's argument and it's the half that's easiest to accept.

In 1588, a year in which Spanish ships of immense number sailed north to conquer Elizabeth's England, Walter Raleigh had an interesting idea, or so it would seem. Then in his forties, a successful member of Parliament, a land owner and soldier with the troubling reputation that he had led the brutal beheadings of innumerable Irishmen and women in the south of Ireland, Raleigh began to finance colonial expeditions, at first primarily to provide himself with tobacco, to which he was reputedly addicted. He had risen upwards in an Elizabethan court that suffered reputations and rewarded brains but this scheme was, on the face of it, absurd. He told Elizabeth he wanted to impress an entire theatre company from London's excellent supply and take it, along with its physical building, to his Virginia Colony and there set it up to profit off the attendance of the native "Inynges" by demanding their payment in the silver and gold that Raleigh had been assured was theirs but which neither he nor any other English adventurer had found.

His colony on Croatan Island had provided his friend and employee, the scientist Thomas Harriott, with this small bit of knowledge; that the local Indians, Croatans and others, were crazy about the white settlers entertainments, fascinated with them much more than they were the muskets and iron balls and skillets the English had brought as trade goods.

And through the colony ran the hope that although Raleigh's fruitless search for gold and silver in Guyana had come to naught, there might still be a chance that the fabled city of El Dorado would be found in the north after all. Raleigh and Harriott reasoned that gold and silver might be extracted from the natives if a large enough entertainment could be devised, but Elizabeth cautioned that the enterprise would have to be carefully hidden from competitors and routed out past the surely northbound Armada.

Speed was faster than the Queen's money and Raleigh, using his own fortune, kidnapped the four remaining actors of the dockside Fyre Cygne Theatre, a mangy collection of rejects from the glossier theatres of London. By night, his men dismantled the structure itself; a circular, but much smaller version of Shakespeare's famous Globe. They numbered each board and beam for reassembly on Croatan and, stowing all on board a Raleigh-owned ship, sailed quietly off to the New World.

Another, darker aspect of Rick Shakespeare's theory has to do with the reputed alchemical skills of Harriott and Raleigh and their imagined "School of the Night." Was the Fyre Cygne Theatre to be set upon a greased spool and whirled around by the recoil of numerous cannons loaded with gunpowder, the actors within frozen into poses that changed slightly with time as what spectators were not blown to smithereens might see as the "movynge pictures" famously mentioned in the play? Rick Shakespeare says he is "researching the possibility."

What is known is that Raleigh's accounts for the succeeding years showed growing profits of New World tobacco, an herb that he largely popularized to a London public eager for thrills.

One of Harriot's scientific tasks as assigned by Raleigh, (and perhaps inspired by John Dee) was to find the optimum stacking for cannon balls on the deck of the ship Tabac. The rolling of the deadly balls on the storm-tossed deck may well have led Harriott to find some use of them as a kind of ball-bearing which would let the stage of the Fyre Cygne Theatre revolve quickly without the use of gunpowder; water power would have been sufficient to spin the already circular structure. Rick Shakespeare conjectures that gunpowder explosions and squibs would then have been used to light the whirling stage from the inside, so spectators would see the actors in blurs of animated flashings. The patent absurdity of this idea seems completely lost on him. Every scholar in the field begs to differ with him.

## V

Darlene Yuc A'Amoto, in particular, begs to differ. The diminutive scholar from Brown was Rick Shakespeare's student, assistant and collaborator in the early years of his rebirth as a scholar, but broke with him upon publication of her small but controversial book: Anythynge He Wants To, The Big Fat Lie. Not surprisingly, it accuses Rick Shakespeare of actually writing the bulk of not only emendations to the manuscript, but possibly the entire work itself. She is the only other person besides Rick Shakespeare to have seen the Groot trunk and its contents. Everything was snatched away from her when he dissolved their collaboration, suddenly turned on her and began threatening legal action. He refuses to this day to let her or anyone else examine the contents, the manuscript or anything else.

"I hate him," she told me. "He's just making it all up."

"He's an odd one, sure enough," I said.

"Odd? Odd? Are you crazy? He's duplicitous and sneaky and a liar and I hate him. He threatened to sue me. Me!"

We were drinking Bloody Marys at a small Jalama Beach bar on the central coast of California. Far off across the water, you could just make out the peaks of the Bleak Islands. Jalama is isolated, only one road in and one road out, with a small campground known mostly by surfers. Darlene Yuc A'Amoto lives there in a tiny tent-camper with three dogs and a pet lizard. She is on an unexplained leave of absence from her professorship in Fresno, an inland city directly east of Jalama Beach. Her life has been ruined, she says, by Rick Shakespeare.

"At first, all was well," she says, lighting a cigarette and staring out to sea. "He can be quite charming when he wants to, did I mention that?"

I said I'd met him and indeed, that was true. I mentioned that I'd also researched the story of the finding of the trunk and that the gun was confirmed by the entire crew.

"Don't tell him that," she cautioned. "He'll hunt you down and probably kill you and feed your body to sharks or whatever it is out there that eats human cadavers."

I said that probably a lot of fish would eat dead anything. I didn't think fish were too picky. I stared out to sea, wondering exactly where Burial Rock was.

"Well, you get my point," she said sharply. "Anyway, he probably hired actors to pretend to be the sailors. I wouldn't put it past him. He's a dangerous son of a bitch. He stole all my research. He used me."

"Do you want to get something to eat? The little campground store has something called Oil Burgers. Are they any good?"

"They're oily, which isn't necessarily a bad thing. Anyway, don't bother. I'll fix something later."

Jalama Beach is the site of natural oil seeps from the Monterey Formation. It is both beautiful and wild but its beach can be studded with occasional oil balls. Darlene Yuc A'Amoto points out in her book that those seeps could well be the inspiration for the many references to oil in the existing manuscripts of "Anythynge You Want To," if you buy her thesis that Rick Shakespeare has concocted much of it.

She blew smoke out of her lips and lungs. She tapped her fingers on the little table.

"Ok," I said. "Look, is there anything to the passages in 'Anythynge You Want To' that seem to point toward the existence of motion pictures? You know what I mean?"

"I know what you mean."

"Well? Have you found any evidence anywhere, any hint that the Sixteenth Century might have had photographic skills unmentioned in any literature that's come down to us?"

"You mean beyond what he's made up and fabricated? No, my answer would be no. As it would be the answer for everyone else in the field whom he hasn't paid off or intimidated. Even David Hockney doesn't believe it." I thought for a minute. Out on the water, waves thundered and seagulls wheeled and shrieked.

"Did you have an affair with Rick Shakespeare? Did it get to that?"

"I wouldn't call it an affair."

"What would you call it?"

"A disaster. A nightmare. You get my point."

"I get your point."

The mystery that is Rick Shakespeare is certainly not solved, nor will it be soon,

I think. I peered out at the water, wondering if the Bleak Islands might be clever constructions of Hollywood, whether he himself might be as constructed as a film script.

Briefly, her hand brushed mine.

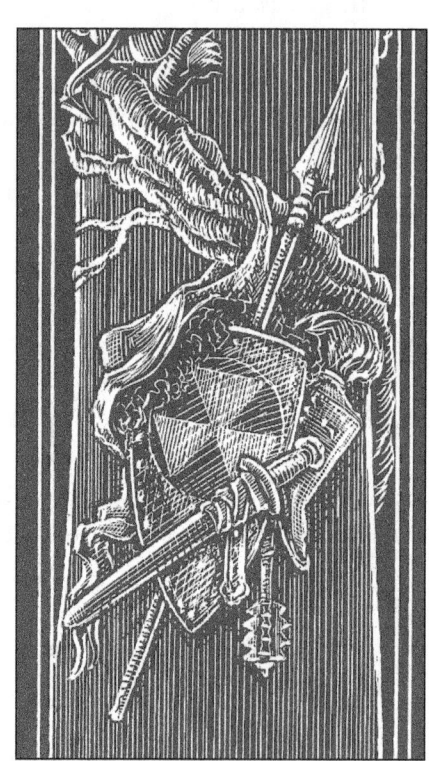

**RICK SHAKESPEARE**, *Hollywood, Summer of Love-In*

# SHAKESPEARE AT SEA!

Rick Shakespeare, balding and bearded, looking remarkably like his famous ancestor, William, waited for me at the top of the gangplank leading onto his yacht, "Tem-Pest II" docked at the Monterey Marina. It was a "Da Vinci Code" moment for me, because, on the spanking clean, if inky black vessel there awaited a literary prize that, if genuine, could change the course of Shakespearian scholarship.

Over thirty years ago, while diving off the Bleak Islands, Rick claims to have stumbled over the remains of The Gilded Hind, an Elizabethan craft, lost in a Pacific storm around 1610. Going for the gold, Rick spent months uncovering the remains of the ship.

Strangely, the "gold" he discovered was a small but priceless library of poetry and drama, once the property of the "Hind's" owner, one Capt. McDucke.

Most important among the volumes, kept sealed in an airtight silver chest, was an original, nearly complete manuscript of "Anythynge You Want To," the long-missing play often attributed to William Shakespeare.

Since I and my fellow Firesign Theatre actors were planning another selected performance from this quasi-mystical comedy, a viewing of the original script would not only be a rare privilege but might also help to solve some of the dramaturgical problems associated with the play's text, hitherto assembled from the many other bits and pieces used by actors and ripped off by other lesser writers and unscrupulous Bankside publishers in Shakespeare's time.

Looking fit, if silvered by the years and worn smooth by his lifetime in the water, Rick welcomed me aboard. He had agreed to let me examine a copy of "Anythynge," which remains in his possession after years of litigation, along with some volumes from Capt. McDucke's library.

Imagine the thrill when seeing such a collectable possible Shakespearian artifact, possibly with corrections and additions in someone's (the author's?) hand. A page of it lay before me, there on the wine-dark ebony desk in Rick's below-decks office. In cramped Elizabethan typography I could make out the (much annotated) beginning of "Anythynge"'s Act I, scene ii:

*"A Nawful Place, upon the heath at dawn. Three Cookes doth the broth spoil.*

> *Cke I Com coking cusines, stok the peet*
> *Bile the ale & the meet be beet*
>
> *Cke II Ive fowl deepfired, a buket's load*
>
> *Cke III Add's 'pleen of Banker, hand of Coppe*
> *Tongue of Lawier, dearly bowt*
>
> *Cke I All must steethe & bile with lava*
> *Whilest we take Five for mokajava."*

"It isn't well known, Dave," said Rick, "but I wrote a lot of original dialog for that big Pflegmish Raadio production of "Anythynge," based on this book. They wanted Shakespeare, they got me!"

His was yet another gloss on the indestructible "lost comedie," which has survived reconstructions by Orson Welles, Noel Coward, The Living Theatre, the cheerfully athletic team of Olivier and Kaye at Stratford in 1951, and of course, by me and my Firesign Theatre partners.

One of us had picked up a dilapidated copy of an 1898ish printing of "Anythynge" back in the "Dear Friends" radio days. Always on the lookout for classic material we incorporated favorite scenes from "Anythynge" into our live act, along with Hemlock Stones' "Giant Rat of Sumatra" and Edmund Dante's "The Count of Monte Cristo." (We reserved William Burroughs and "Winnie The Pooh" for live radio.)

Much later, at the beginning of a brief revival of radio plays in the 1980s, "Anythynge" got one of those elaborate European productions only possible on state-supported radio. HRH the Queen herself attended that celebrated live broadcast, at least until an early luncheon arrived during the endless retakes of Act 1, Scene Two.

Rick refused to identify his contributions to the Pflegmish radio play, although I suspect the Prologue ("O for a microphone and wire," it begins) to be in his "slight of hand."

The entire experience aboard the "Tem-Pest II" remains one of my Favorites Among the Famous, along with weighing the once-golden Oscar® for "Casablanca," shaking the shaking hand of the lyricist of "Tea For Two," and taking over the all-night radio production watch from Norman Corwin, the guy who pretty much invented what it is I do.

"Now, you know the whole book is in my safe-deposit box in Switzerland. This is the only page I let anybody see in the original, because it was loose when I found it and it had a bunch of writing on it. I think it was the Captain's, taking notes on tropical nights when the ship was becalmed. This one here says 'Brotherhood of Kappa Delta' and then 'three humors only' when the Weird Cookes come in."

"Very philosophical."

"Oh, that's the thing, Dave. At the bottom of the whole 'comedie' is a big alchemical formula that only the truly Metaphysically Adept can figure out. You know the scene where Marie says 'What's Alchemie to me, or me to Alchemie? Must I repeat this formula anon?'"

"And the Bishop replies 'Absolutely, Sweet Marie. Tis wizzard's fun!' Then they talk about changing mice from lead to gold?"

"They could do that. They took the little lead mice they used for fishing and charged them up with golden power so that if you had one you could get girls horny or blow things up, whatever. There's a formula for it in one of the Captain's collection right here, 'Booke of Cerebral Magicks.' I don't open it up, because it might get damaged and anyway, a lot of it is pretty much double-X-rated."

"Really?"

"Well, Dave, really, what is reality anyway? 'Anythynge You Want To,' right?"

"Unless everything you know is wrong."

Rick held up two more leather-bound books, "Here's another from the Captain's library, 'Plotinus The Mad' by Christopher Marlow, and this one's 'Ye Trajedy of Young Candidus' by Comedon and Greene. I think he may have done performances aboard ship from these plays."

"Wow! Imagine doing that scene where the ship goes down in a huge tempest in a real tempest!"

"Very existential, man!"

We gave each other manly hugs and, well, maybe the visit wasn't as good as sharing the stage with media greats George Tirebiter, Bebop Lobo, Ralph Spoilsport and The Wizard of Oz, but it was right up there.

And the next time you see us, The Firesign Theatre will be playing its justly renowned version of "Anythynge You Want To," sillier than ever, because of my brief encounter with Shakespeare's great, great, etc. grand nephew, Rick.

# LOCATION JOTTINGS
## By Derrick Escrow & Rick Shakespeare

The following was discovered in a fax to Phil Proctor Productions dated April 15th, 1996. Old show business friends of Proctor's, Escrow and Shakespeare were working together once again on the set of "Lethal Attraction," a version of "Othello" set in East L. A. Shakespeare had been called in to provide additional dialogue. Proctor recalls his own "lethal attraction" to computer games, the probable source of this material. It would appear that Escrow interpolated the lines in brackets in irritation over his tax bill, which was due that day. A subsequent fax, dated June 7th, eliminated those lines and credited "the long lost Wired Quarto as read by Frank Funtt" as the source.

*CD or not CD, that is the question.*
*Whether tis easier in the game*
*To surf through the slings and arrows of*
*Sonic Hedgehog, or to fake harm against a*
*Siege of Pacmen and by opposing, eat them.*
*To buy, to keep; buy more!*
*And buying more, to say we end the*
*Wrist ache and the thousand toaster flocks*
*That flap across a screen of blue,*
*For an animation directly out of MYST.*
*To buy — to charge! Ay, join the club.*
*For from that CD Rom what bills may come*
*When we have shutted off computer's power*
*Puts us on pause. [That's the interface that*
*Makes Macintosh of so long life.*
*For who'd not products buy*
*That interact with software sold,*
*But that the need of paying out —*
*"Plus tax" to Inca Sam's collector, who's*
*unfair share no one enough can earn —*

*Probates our will and makes us*
*Rather pay the bills we have*
*Than run up others for some IBM.]*
*Thus, Bill Gates makes consumers of us all!*
*And corporations new, in revolution,*
*Are taken o'er with the lowest bid*
*To manufacturers of great chips!*
*And in a moment, at his regard,*
*Transistors burn and fry*
*And Intel's — out of action.*

**Pencil Sketch of Dr. Firesign's Theatre of the Plains**
Anonymous Artiste © Zachariah Archive

# THE LEGEND OF "THE FIRESIGN THEATRE"

By Uline Blogger and E. M. Ailer
Elmertown State Historical Assoc., L. P.

### THE FIRST AMERICAN THEATRE 1889-1906

It would be more than two centuries after the Puritan Elision and the shredding of playbooks for better insulation during the Little Glacial Era that unexpected texts distantly related to Shakesphere's Lost Comedy, "Anythynge You Want To," began to re-emerge in the traveling Medicine Shows of the West, notably in raw, organic farce.

The visit in 1889[358] of a "Dr. Firesign's Antique Theatre of the Plains and Eclectic[359] Buffalo Show" to the Forth of Julee Exposition in Elmer County, Nebraska, appears to begin an American tradition of clowning and Art that may seem bewildering because of the variety and complex relationships among the men who have performed under the various banners of the Theatre.

This traveling Medicine Show sold a product called Olde Bombaye Opium Restorative[360] and, we know, thanks to one of the actor's scripts, discovered among the effects of a retired gunfighter[361] in Plano, Texas, that they performed a highly abbreviated version of the classic French farce-drama, *The Count of Monte Christo*,[362] to entertain and entice the "marks" to buy.

---

[358] Mentioned but briefly in General Custer's *Western States Journal* for 1890, as part of a report on cattle wrestling in the southern North Dakota town of Bent.

[359] Posters advertising a "Electric Burralo Balancing Act" apparently are misprints.

[360] "Balls For the Ladies! Balm For the Men!" proclaims an early advertising poster for this probably mildly hallucinogenic cure-all.

[361] Known as The Zachariah Kid, he was an occasional community theatre actor after retiring with Matthew, his range partner of many years, to manage a gay Dude's Ranch in Curio, Arizona. As a boy, Zachariah left an oppressive home-life to join the entertainers appearing at the Elmer County 4th of July Bonfire and Anvil Shoot. According to Zach, "Dr. Benjamin Firesign" was actually Dr. Bernard Gumm, a dentist (who gave "opium on request" as the sign in his window read), and had somehow been hired to stage the "living frieze" Pageant of America. Zach later became a card-shark and member of The Crackers Band; the Firesign Theatre, described in Zach's diaries as a "repertoire confidence team," evolved into the Fried Chicken Insurance Co. and briefly ran the town of Carnage, Nebraska.

[362] If you have read this book up to this point, you will realize that this play is not the same as the epic melodrama that starred Eugene O'Neil's sainted father.

*Kansas chicken-runner "Honest Abe Bowman" aka "Dr. Firesign." Elmertown, Nebraska, 1890.*

Further, we have discovered that the Antique Theatre had been organized only a short time before by one "Honest Abe" Bowman — a promoter and Kansas chicken-runner who assumed the name "Dr." Firesign.[363] Bowman was born in Ohio, near Sod Shack, in 1864.

---

[363] "Firesign" in this case seems to have roots in alchemical cant, which suited Bowman's character as a fearless salesman. The show wagon, with its drop-leaf stage and Firesign name in gold-leaf, had come out of the West, along the Platte River Valley, and assumed instant interest when it appeared in the dark of night at the Main Gate of Ft. Nowhears, Neb. Some thought Indians might have brought it to the Fort just to get rid of it, others felt it was haunted(!). It was army surplus property in 1888 and purchased by Abe Bowman, who seems to have thought of a profitable use for it.

His partner in this venture was the charming, sometime chemist[364] and full-time Romantic, Marshall Archer, who specialized in playing the elderly character parts both on and off the stage, to the considerable amusement of the local dames. Archer was possibly born in Arkansas around 1866.[365]

Bowman and Archer recruited two other performers, Leo Rothman and Albright Ames (known here as "Harry Ames Sr."). Rothman was only seventeen when he was stranded with a company of the ever-popular melodrama, *Buckboard Virtue*, in St. Louis in 1889. The Antique Theatre was headed north to Nebraska, and Rothman joined rather than chance a trip back across the rugged heartland to his home in New York City's immigrant ghetto.

"Harry" Ames, Sr., eldest of the four (known as "Harry," he was born in Boomingtown, Indiana in 1863), had already worked the West for several years with his own rival company of *The Count*. He played leading roles, repaired the wagons and shoed the horses if necessary.

During the Gay Nineties, as the "medicine" side of the Theatre gave way to the "show" side; magic, balloon acts and especially the hermetic Apache entertainment known as "buffalo balancing" were added to the ever-popular Count, *Anythynge You Want To* (still thought to have been written by Shakespeare!) and, after a woman was available to the cast, *Orphan's Tears, or Buckboard Virtue Rewarded*.[366]

A principal attraction of the troupe was an American bison named King Arthur, and known as "Art."[367] Young Rothman became Art's special friend and confidant, and was desolated by the beast's sudden death (of congestion) in 1900.[368]

---

[364] Archer "cooked" the medicines, including "Chief Knockout's Pyramid Pushover Paste" and "Don Brujaja's Inca Hell Oil Tonic." In an extraordinary feat of legerdemain, climaxing a tent show in Curio, Arizona, Archer toasted the "brave and bully boys of Arizona Territory" and suddenly was transformed into a large, silver crow which rose like a shot and soared away.

[365] Although there are other schools of thought, many of them espoused by the tenured staff of Another School of Thought and Metaphysics in Coldfoot, Massachusetts.

[366] The part of Uncle Field Marshal Thomas Lagree Quadroon was played in blackface. Roy Rogers and Dale Evans used this hoary script as the basis for "Rangeland Romance" (1942) with Stepin Fetchit in the role. The woman who briefly joined the original quartet, Beaulabelle Latourneau, was the wife of a Nebraska banker and an amateur actress with the Kearney Light Opera. Enamored of Leo, she bankrolled the tour of mining towns along the Colorado River during which a series of studio portraits were taken and preserved by Needles, California photographer P. Bauregard, inventor of the sepiatone process. Pop culturalist Harry Cox claims to own a "wire recording" of a performance of *Orphan's Tears*, seen (and heard!) in his film, *Everything You Know Is Wrong* (1975).

[367] Rothman liked to say he was "doing art for Art's sake."

[368] The creature was stuffed and presented to Buffalo Bill's Museum and Ranch, where it remained for many years with a billboard showing how Leo, to the delight of tent-show audiences, could make the great beast so effortlessly "weightless."

*Leo Rothman (1872-1956) as Edmund Dantes in
"The Count of Monte Cristo," San Francisco, 1901.*

Soon after, Rothman left Dr. Firesign and returned to New York after he was offered a chance to appear as a comedy "Mammy" singer with the knockabout Klein Brothers,[369] then a vaudeville phenomenon.

Troubled by the loss of their bison and tired of touring, "Dr. Firesign's Theatre" was disbanded in San Francisco early in 1901. Archer, Bowman and Ames kept in

---

[369] A zany music publishing, song writing and show-stopping team that entertained millions for the first fifty years of the 20th century, the Rothman & Klein partnership was founded on Leo Rothman's (1872-1956) astonishing skill as a performer of the songs, and in musical shows written by composer Sammy Klein (1871-1939), his lyricist brother Georgie (1872-1946) and their younger brother "Hap," a comedian-patriot (1875-1951). The three were sometimes joined by their stepbrother Hamilton "Hammy" Klein (1881-1969) who later capered independently on his own Westinghouse Network variety show, *Hot Time Tonight!* A totally fictionalized biography of the team was filmed as *The Rothman & Klein Story* (MRM, 1940, re-released in 1951 as *Our Finest Hours*).

touch with Leo by mail, and the three saw one another almost daily in the Tenderloin, where they ate. Ames married in 1902 and his wife, the former Lurlene DiAngelo,[370] had a son they named Harry, Jr. in that same year.

Bowman and Archer decided not to join Ames in his new "Nickel-Odeon" business, but to try their hands at "legitimate" theatrical production. In 1903, after a string of flops,[371] Ames came to them with the manuscript of Emilio Bombardillo's only opera, *The Floating Prince*, and offered to back it. Bombardillo had been the Ames' housemate for some time by then and had been "brushing it up" in the front parlor, sometimes late at night. Unexpected success was immediate and a long run and world-wide rights broght prosperity to all concerned.

With Ames as General Manager, the trio built the gracious, Edwardian "Firesign Opera House" at the corner of Boat and Gold in the notorious Prong Street District. It opened February 13, 1904 with a new production of *The Floating Prince*, to which Bombardillo had added the lilting "Revenge Duet" and the still-popular Edison cylinder hit, "The Saloon Song."[372] The opera enjoyed renewed success and was revived thirty-eight times during the next two years.

Shortly after the opening, Archer engaged the young English actor, Hemlock Stones, who had only recently returned from a fearful and disappointing tour of Java, the Banana Straits and Dutch East Sumatra. As "Hamlock, Prince of Venice,"

---

[370] When she married Harry Ames, Sr., Lurlene DiAngelo was the fifteen-year-old daughter of recent Italian immigrants, Yodo and Maria DiAngelo. Back home, in their native Sardinia, in the little village of Fettucini, two families had lived side-by-side for centuries. In the big "Casa Manoria" lived the Bombardillos, scourge of the Ravioli district of Parma, famous as the "cheese town." Next door, in the modest little "Lavatorio," lived the humble DiAngelos. They had always done everything the Bombardillos told them to do and were relatively happy. Upon Lurlene's birth in 1887, she had been instantly betrothed (according to ancient Fettucini custom) to her next-door-neighbor, the 65-year-old Emilio Bombardillo, who was then at the end of a long and dazzling European operatic career (as a tenor), and had recently turned to composing and conducting. During one of his Farewell Tours, Lurlene's family emigrated secretly to San Francisco, seeking a better life for themselves and their ten-year-old daughter. In her fifteenth year, a beauty by all accounts, she fell in love with the thirty-nine-year-old Ames and settled into a happy and fecund life with him until his death in 1927. Lurlene herself lived until her one-hundredth year at the elegant Ames Estate on Commercial Street, where she entertained visitors and cooked cheese until her passing in 1987.

[371] They tried *Sherlock's Lost Mystery — The Giant Rat of Sumatra*, with a William Gillette look-alike and no less than three different Dr. Watsons! They couldn't get *My Flying Machine* off the ground. *Count Mosca*, a spy adventure, buzzed off. *It's All About Me!* didn't really have to be about any anything, and wasn't, not even the gloriously full-figured Emmy Bouvine.

[372] Bombardillo was heartbroken by Lurlene's disappearance and had searched for her until, penniless and eighty-years old, he traced her to San Francisco, where he arrived just before her marriage to Ames. *The Floating Prince* had been dashed off for money during a stop at Brighton, on the way. It had been performed (in Italian, under the title *Il Vino Confuso*) by the Brighton Railway Light Opera in 1895. The text was freely adapted from Shakespeare's *Anythynge You Want To*, the only book available to him in his Brighton hotel. Upon arriving in San Francisco, Bombardillo claimed "manorial rights" and moved in with the couple, happily gobbling cheese, penning tunes, gossiping and babysitting during the Ames' frequent trips to Hollywood. He, too, lived to be 100 and died on Father's Day, 1922.

# THE FIRESIGN OPERA HOUSE, SAN FRANCISCO, 1906

*Hemlock Stones (center) as Hamlock, Prince of Venice.*

he delighted San Franciscans with his prowess on the boards, and later delighted them again in newspaper accounts of his amorous exploits with young socialites.[373]

Shortly after, the Irish actor-manager Flynn Shenannigan filled the theatre again and again with his performances of The Porter in *That Scottish Play*, "Dad" in *The Count of Monte Christo* and both Flounder and the Second Grave Digger in *Anythynge You Want To*.

---

[373] As reported in Charles Dudley's *San Francisco Rouser*, a popular sex newspaper of the time and the eventual source of the Charles Foster Dudley millions. Dudley and Stones were to meet again in 1920 in Chicago when the by then Great Defective pursued his American nemesis, "The Electrician" in the case known as "The Fuse of Doom." (Filmed by Raspublic in 1936.)

Fame, however provincial, satisfied Stones (and the others) until 1906 when, fightened by "the biggest bloody earthquake I ever saw!" he leaped from his window at the Top o' the Nob Hotel and headed East.[374]

That disastrous earthquake brought down the Firesign Opera House, completely destroying the building and ending two brilliant years of theatrical success in the City by the Bay City.[375]

## A MOVING AND PICTURESQUE INTERLUDE 1907-1920

Shaken but wealthy, Bowman and Archer moved south to Santa Barbara, a pleasant watering-spot in Southern California, suddenly home to several motion-picture studios and hundreds of starlets.[376] The pair quickly wrote a few silent scenarios, borrowed a "borrowed" Edison camera and ground out the cult-classic serial adventure, Venus In Peril, featuring the frequently under-dressed Venus Dinudo, an early exponent of the curious German cult, "naturism."[377] Harry Ames quickly established a distribution company, Acme Pictures, for the 13-episode serial. Its sole investor was a 38-year-old financial wizard, Jonas Acme.[378]

---

[374] Hemlock Stones returned to England after this traumatic event and took up private practice as a detective. His case, "The Giant Rat of Sumatra," as reported by his friend Sir John Flotsom, O.D. in *The Lancers* (January 1926), includes some references to his South Seas adventures. As noted in a previous note, Stones went to Chicago in pursuit of the missing Zeppelin Tube. His closing words, as transcribed by Sir John, are well worth repeating: "And so, the myth of The Electrician was exploded at last, like his hideous Clockwork Rat-hound, Tojo. My labors now completed, my dear compendium and I return to our sweets at the Holland Daze Inn, thankful that for tonight, Chicagoans might sleep like Crazy Monkeys under an electrical blanket of thick, American combustible violence, er, violins!"

[375] And just to show that the world of Show Biz is totally inter- if not actually related, among the successful productions at the Opera House were two early musical comedy hits with Rothman & Klein scores, *Footprints in the Sky* and *German Spring*.

[376] American Studios, Mission-Mutual and Allied-Cosmo all escaped Hollywood, taking their Edison cameras with them, but declining to pay ten cents a yard for the film forever just for the rights. Santa Barbara was much too far and difficult to get to before the invention of the hired limo in 1922.

[377] Venus was nineteen in 1908 and vigorously pursued by Archer. She eventually spurned his advances. By a curious coincidence, she met and married a sometime silent movie actor named Monte Burke, later owner of Elysia, an early Southern California nudist camp, featured in a sensational skin-flick which allowed Burke to retire young. They are both personalities in George Tirebiter's tale, *The Ronald Reagan Murder Case*.

[378] Acme was from Chicago and had built a solid fortune in the West on the heels of the Chinese influx of the 19th century. The film industry in California was actually started by Yun Sat Hop of Sacramento, who used the flickering light produced by the cracks between fast-moving railroad cars to produce the ephemeral Sino-American films, most of which were committed to memory by elderly Chinese gandy dancers and so lost to modern times. Acme had come West as a robust trackwalker for the Dudley-Pacific Line, having left his Bohemian parents, Yelda and Bohunk Acmenski, in Chicago near the sweltering Pitts

*Mixville Pictures star Venus Dinudo (1912)*

By 1910, Bowman and Archer had traveled still farther south to Hollywood, where they seem to have been involved in the first feature film made there, *The Count of Monte Cristo*, based on a French prison novel related to the Milanese *commedia* by title and little else. They established themselves as Mixville Pictures[379] and located their small studio on Alvarado Street in a charming hillside Mexican suburb of Downtown.[380]

---

District. Acme, hungry, but always ready for a few laughs, was immediately won over by the Chinese filmmakers of Sacramento. Acme invented a technique whereby the delicate "Willow Leaf" pictures could be preserved on thin sheets of California gold, where they would last for up to two days — enough time for Acme to rush them to his burgeoning chain, Goo Luk Chinese Food Company. In 1908, attracted by the rowdy successes of the Firesign Opera House, Acme joined forces with Ames to distribute the cruder Caucasian product and subsequently made a quick fortune by buying up the Dudley newspapers. He returned to Chicago to sit on an Empire that "never came up frowning, but didn't make *some* money!"

379 Mixville Pictures was financed in large part by the above-mentioned Charles Foster Dudley, whose journalistic empire had been snatched from him by the rapacious Jonas Acme machine. In the interim years before he "obtained" his Senate seat, (some say Acme bought it in 1920 to "give poor Dud something to do"), Dudley edited a tiny news-sheet, *The Mixville Rocket*, serving the bi-lingual neighborhood that was once home to Tom Mix, Hot Roach and Bison film studios, all by then abandoned. Improbably, the masthead of the *Rocket* was graced by "Art," the one-time star of the Firesign Theatre of the Plains, whose proud and noble head on an eight-color poster had once impressed Hilario Gomez, the founder of the rag. It seemed only natural for the company to use Art as a mascot for the motion picture business as well.

380 For a complete book-length study of this interesting independent film enterprise, consult *Mixville: Home to Hi Frequency* by Kay Day Tower (Research Books Press, London NJ, 1994)

In 1919, Metro, the fast French newsreel producers, bought out, first Roach, then Mixville, to become Metro-Roach-Mixville.[381] Bowman and Archer, both wealthy and in active middle-age, decided to embark upon a final and sentimental Grand Farewell Tour of The Original Firesign Theatre.

## THE "END" OF THE FIRESIGN THEATRE 1920-1930

The two actor-managers arranged a vaudeville circuit of Latin America featuring their old-fashioned "Buffalo Show" and a punched-up version of The Count. First, they acquired a new bison (one of the last of the Montana Whites) and, after getting Leo Rothman's agreement, they named him "Art." Then, from their stock company of Mixville Pictures actors, two leading men were chosen — Harry Cox and Leo Artunian.[382]

This group, the third incarnation of "The Firesign Theatre," toured Latin America for some five years before becoming involved in the incredible recovery of an unusual map that eventually guided them to the lost Inca Citadel of Shangra Deelitl, then known as Bat City.[383]

It was in this Andean Paradise that the two original Firesigners, Archer and Bowman, were reported to have passed on (in 1928 and 1930 respectively), living their last years spinning stories about their lives which were then woven into distinctive Andean "story belts," a folk craft which persists to this day in spite of efforts to discourage it.

Harry Cox returned to the USA in 1931, became a lumber executive in Clearcut,

---

[381] Between 1929 and 1933, massive corporate battles cleared the way for MRM's merger with the talkie giant, 20th Century Paranoid. The conglomerate was then known as Paranoid Pictures and dominated the industry through the 1940's and '50's, along with Goldwyn, Mertz Bros., Allied Artistes and Perry-Mutual. In 1956 Paranoid was sold to the Yamoto Brothers of Japan and devoted itself to thrilling Atomic Monster movies like *Gorgonzola The Cheese Monster*. Ironically, "Artu Burrulu," the company mascot, has become a familiar Japanese folk figure, beloved by children.

[382] Years later, Harry Cox said that he and Artunian were chosen not so much for their acting skills as for their drug habits! He claimed that both were at the time addicted to "mary jane" and had been initiated into that peculiar fraternity which still plagues much of South America, "*Los Amigos Del Muerte*," a semi-penitential clan of religious criminals and rodent worshipers which has never, to this day, done anything anybody wanted it to.

[383] Through their *hermanos* in *Los Amigos*, Cox and Artunian had access to the sacred Routo de los Gods, the fabled astral highway believed to stretch invisibly from Alaska to Peru. This quaint belief had evidently captured the fancy of Bowman and Archer (Archer, it will be remembered had experienced a vision of Don Brujaja as an ancient cockroach wearing a sombrero in Curio), both of whom told the Los Angeles *Daily Buzz* that they were going to "catch Mescalito at the top of the hill." Since there were no hipsters and only jazz buffs smoked "the weed," practically no one understood a word of their story. See Appendix Fourteen!

Oregon and, in 1936, founded the International Funny Names Clubs of America, Inc., which he led for twelve years.[384]

Leo Artunian came down from the Andes sometime in the 1940's "looking like a long-haired llama" and was last seen on a bamboo raft, traveling toward the Devil's Triangle in 1947.[385]

## THE FIRESIGN RADIO THEATRE 1939-1942

Albright "Harry" Ames, a member of the original "Theatre of the Plains" had produced Cohen's comedy *The Keys to Baldpate* in 1914 and was a partner in the Knox-Haymarket circuit until 1930, when he bought his first mid-Western broadcasting station, WOP in Chicago. A victim of early dementia, Ames lived in seclusion until 1946, protected by his wife, Lurlene. Their daughter, Lurlene Jr. eventually became known as the Broadway and film star Lillie LaMont.[386] She married young Chicago radio actor George Tirebiter[387] in 1941.

Harry, Jr. managed his father's theatre circuit in the early Thirties and developed a popular movie house intermission entertainment he called "The Dr. Blowjob Show," which helped out-of-work people all over the country win small prizes and feel better. He later developed a popular following as "Major Arcana"[388] and presented amateur contests in the South and Midwest.

Thus, the son of one of the founders of The Firesign Theatre was destined to initiate its next incarnation, which can be dated to 1939 and superlative company assembled in Chicago for the Firesign Radio Theatre.

---

384 His son, Sylvester "Happy Harry" Cox was born in 1925. His mother was the former Lorna Porter, a timber heiress. Harry's sister Mamie was Surrealist Presidential candidate George Papoon's mother. In the late 1960's, "Happy Harry" started Nude Age Enterprises and went on to become a celebrated pop newshound, mythbuster and producer of the "Everything You Know Is Wrong About . . ." television series.

385 An "odd couple" indeed were pot-addicts Cox and Artunian. Apparently they had nothing else in common but the "jumbles." Artunian became a Universal Seeker of The Truth, only to vanish into the Sub-Consciousness of Nothingness. Cox, who could fugue derivatives to ten decimals in his head, enjoyed computing premiums and neglected his son who became a pilot for the US Air Mail Corps. The elder Cox died in 1948 in the midst of solving the so-called "Devil's Conundrum," a calculation requiring an infinite number of steps.

386 This Lillie Lamont may be the same "Lila Lomond" who appeared in many silent quickies of the late 1920's with the original Leroy The Dog. There were eighty-odd shorts, all in questionable taste, made by the notorious Fireoscope-Mutosign Company. She attained conventional stardom in Rothman & Klein's stage revue *Vandals of 1934*.

387 Tirebiter has written of their relationship in *The Ronald Reagan Murder Case*, BearManor Books, 2007.

388 Ames broadcast "Major Arcana's Aboriginal Amateur Hours" for many years and was producer/director of the popular soap-opera, "End of Song!" (1938-1945). He was a perennial award-winner for his syndicated radio shorts, "The Forward Into the Past Cavalcade of Events."

*An astounded winner of the "Major Arcana Amateur Hour" helped to his feet by Joe Beets and Dwight Yeast. Harry Ames is at right.*

With Harry Ames directing and providing the essential link to the past, the Radio Theatre was produced by veteran Chicago radio man Joe Beets[389] and written by the enormously talented young actor/dramatist, George Leroy Tirebiter[390] (then only nineteen and not yet married to Lillie). With the Radio Theatre, "Georgie" wrote such often frightening and always heartwarming programs as "Shoes For Industry," "Firesign Chats of 1940" and "Anytown USA." An early hit was their Thanksgiving special, "Pass The Indian, Please."

According to Tirebiter,[391] he, Beets and Ames acquired the trademark rights to "Firesign Theatre" from the Rothman & Klein Group, along with the literary rights to "Nick Danger," a fictional character dating back to the 1880's, early in 1940.[392]

---

[389] Beets had the distinction of broadcasting the first "remote" radio news report in 1921! He was later a member of the celebrated Radio Team which welcomed Lindburgh home from Paris.

[390] George's later adventure as Surrealist Vice Presidential candidate in 1976 has been detailed in *Dr. Firesign's Follies*, BearManor Media, 2008.

[391] In the detailed program notes for The Firesign Theatre's *Box of Danger* (Shout! 2008)

[392] Some scholars maintain that Hemlock Stones was twice a father in the USA. His first illegitimate offspring may have been the child of one Matilda "Maudie" Briggs, a shipowner's "wild daughter," whom Stones had brought back to San Francisco from the South Seas. Maudie bore him a son, but could not bear his "Englished" ways and fled with a local businessman, the aforementioned Jonas Acme. Acme never knew

## ADVERTISEMENT, CIRCA 1910

Lem Pozzo, a penny-a-word pulp writer for *Spicy Mystery* was the occasional *nom-de-plume* of screenwriter and novelist F. Scott Firestone, who claimed to have a drinking buddy named "Dick Danger,"[393] on whom he based his highly stylized version of "Nick Danger" in a slew of stories and novelettes including "Men In Hats," which became the first episode in the "Danger"[394] series.

Other members of the mercurial theatre were Ames' sister Lillie, now a little "mature" for the yearly *Vandals*, but an instant hit in George's suspenseful "Phone Trouble;" Ed Edmunds (in real life a full-blooded Navaho Indian, known as Eddie Soaring Eagle back on the Rez); and two well known studio actors, Ffloyd Damme and Chester Allan Arthur.[395]

Successful in their first year with clever propaganda plays, mostly in verse, Ames and Tirebiter decided to "get more commercial" and, starting in their 1941 season,

---

who was the father of the child, and placed it in the orphanage attached to a Greek Orthodox monastery in the little village of Dangor, Maine, just across Krank's Bay from scenic Nig Island, which Acme had just purchased with hoarded Chinese gold. The monastery's records were unearthed in 1973 and a "Nicola Dangoropolis" was admitted in 1901, his sponsor recorded as J. Acme. Some historians identify this boy with the actual (or "real") private detective hero "Nick" (sometimes "Dick") "Danger," whose exploits had long been fictionalized in pulp magazines.

**393** It's also possible the name might have been a joke on the popular "Dick Private, Private Dick" comic strip of the time.

**394** Hemlock Stones' second illegitimate son may have been the child born in 1922, in Chicago, to one Miss Eleanor Roosevelt, the daughter of Yoko and Solomon Rosenfelt. Miss Roosevelt later married an older man who took pity on her, a local German butcher named Adolph Riefenbissen. The child, named George Tirebiter (a customs agent had translated the family name) was reared as the couple's natural son. Adolph, an unsophisticated "*fiecht-wurgler*" thought babies came out of tin cans. If Tirebiter's father was indeed Hemlock Stones he was doubly blood-linked to the Original Firesign Theatre. (Blood-links, or *blootwurst* is what Adolf *wurgled* out of pigs. Miss Eleanor Roosevelt, who was widowed in 1940, should not be confused with the other one.)

**395** Ffloyd Damme went on to be a popular commercial announcer and a voice for the Future Faire's Bozo Bus Ride. "Chesty" Arthur served as a Major General in the United Snakes Propaganda Service and later with "Wild Bull" Casey of the Office of Secret Facts. He was an active local "dive bomber" until his death at 95 in Hurricane Alice.

**"Nick Danger" cast, CBS, 1942. l to r: "Chesty" Arthur, Ed Edmunds, Harry Ames, George Tirebiter**

"The Firesign Mystery Theatre" was born, along with the most popular radio detective of them all, Nick Danger, whose adventures only lasted one season — 1941-42.[396]

The title role of Nick was portrayed by Ed Edmunds, while Ames directed and played Nick's radio nemesis, Sgt. (later Lt.) Alvin Bradshaw. Lillie doubled as Nick's secretary Ruth and his sometime girlfriend, Nancy. Tirebiter capered through the brief run in various obstreperous character parts he wrote for himself, while Damme and Arthur alternated as villains. The sound effects man was Tony LaRosa and the announcer Dwight Yeast.[397]

When the President declared war over the solution of Nick's thirteenth radio adventure,[398] the series came to an end. Young Eddie Soaring Eagle joined the Air Forces and became a celebrated "Ace." When his "Spitter" was reported lost over Micronesia in 1944, the Allied World mourned.[399]

---

[396] A season plagued by problems, reports Tirebiter, after which he left the series for CBS and "Hollywood Madhouse," starring himself and his recently married spouse, Lillie Ames LaMont.

[397] Yeast attached himself to the Danger program and has joined it as announcer in every revival. His Canadian Radio Union Card is #007.

[398] Titled "Cut 'em Off At The Past," the program was brutally parodied by a later incarnation of Firesign as *How Can You Be In Two Places At Once?*

[399] The legend of Eddie Soaring Eagle was never stilled, of course. Scholarship does indeed support the contention that Eddie did not die, as reported by the military. The book *Soaring Eagle Above, China*

*W. C. Fields and George Tirebiter, "Hollywood Madhouse."*

Harry Ames Jr., made Signal Corps films for the Duration. He became a minor Hollywood producer, going into television movies in the late 1950's.[400]

Joe Beets, who had organized the patriotic *Shoes For Industry War Revue*, toured both theatres of action. Later, television welcomed him like no other hero and awarded him Thursday night and a place in America's heart. The Genial "Crying Clown of Hollywood" retired in 1971 and immediately passed away in his sleep at his estate "A Knight's Rest" in Yucaipa, California.

Of course, George Tirebiter, the toast of American radio, won Hollywood contracts at both Paranoid Pictures and CBS and celebrated five years of network success with "Hollywood Madhouse"[401] His first film for Paranoid, co-written with F. Oliver Tulley, was the trench musical *Babes In Khaki* (1942) which revived Lillie's career in the sentimental role of a battlefield entertainer whose sergeant boyfriend has just been sent on a dangerous mission.

---

*Below* (Ransome House 1971) by Bradford Shaw, Lt. Col. (Ret.), rather successfully proves that Eddie and the great Chinese comic figure of the revolution, Yang Pow Yin (White Flying Cloud), are one and the same.

[400] Notably *Hawaiian Sellout!* (1956-1961), *Punter's Girls*, starring Flip Punter (1961-1966), *Eva and Der Schnifter* (1963-1965), and *Carhook!* (1965-66). All were aired on PBS, the Paranoid Broadcasting System, of which Ames was a vice-president.

[401] It is likely that George's "hot-crossed" romance with Lillie brought about his eventual downfall. One must remember that George was not yet twenty-one and just a millionaire. Lillie, whom many had called a has-been when she left the Broadway stage, was nearly thirty-eight and, though still glamorous, a heavy drinker. It has been surmised that their marriage was engineered by Eleanor Tirebiter, George's domineering mother

"The Firesign Theatre" and "Nick Danger" trademarks returned to Rothman & Klein in 1950 as part of a divorce settlement with Lillie. Tirebiter created his own radio detective[402] and played him for a year, until he was blacklisted by his ex-wife, now retired to a hotel bungalow in Santa Barbara.

In 1953, with the appearance of Rock & Roll Kings like "Little" Elvis, "Fats" Chequers and "Dumps" Domino, the world of entertainment changed, never to appear the same again, even if one wanted it to; and it certainly seemed that the "original" Firesign Theatre was also gone forever.

## FIRESIGN FRANCHISES

In that great R&B year, only Leo Rothman from the long-forgotten Theatre of the Plains was still alive. At eighty-one, he had to completely change his musical thinking and, haltingly, began to write the popular hits for which he is primarily remembered today. Writing with Yammy and Beepo, the grandsons of Hammy Klein, he finally created the stupendous crossover-chart-topper "(These) Foolish Hands," recorded by The Flat Notes on the old Cobra label in the basement of a Memphis record store.[403]

Rothman himself had fathered a son in 1930, after his marriage to a beauty from the Harlem Cotton Cuties, Miss Apricot Brown. The boy was named Doctor Leo Rothman, after Dr. Elmer Doctor, a close family friend. In 1957, greased by his

---

and that "Georgie" went through with it to please her. Eleanor, widowed in 1940, moved in with Harry Ames and married him in a double ceremony with Lillie and George in Las Vegas in 1941. To everyone's surprise, Eleanor and Ames were very happy and their son Harry III, a jolly little boy, was born the next year.

402 "Maxwell Morgan, Crime Cabby," based on a *noir* novel by Conrad Wyrich and Tirebiter's screenplay, *Morgan For Hire* (Flintrige Films, 1948).

403 *Memphis Moonlight* (Abu Dhabi/Universal 2008) tells the story of the recording of this and several other Cobra hits, with Abe Vigoda as Rothman.

***"Oz" Brinkman at Elysian Fields, 1967***

elderly pater's success, "Doc" got a job in radio, featuring the new R&B sounds and by 1960 he was the hottest entrepreneur of R&B acts in the world.

In 1968, after selling his organization to MRM for 3.5 million, "Doc" declared he was giving up all his gold records and other possessions and moving to Japan to start a music and comedy television network, UTV. Joining with him in his new venture were two other descendants of the 19th century Firesign, George Tirebiter and his half-brother Harry Ames III.[404]

Coincidentally, in 1967, a popular L.A. AM radio nighthawk, Oz Brinkman, bought a used copy of the long out-of-print "Rothman & Klein Radio Sketchbook," which contained scripts for "Nick Danger,"[405] real Western adventure tales with

---

[404] Born in 1942 and thus 22 years younger than the 48-year-old Tirebither.

[405] There is, at this point, another story that concerns the "true" identity of "Nick Danger." Lem Potzo, who wrote the pulp adventures of "Nick Danger" for various Rothman & Klein *Dime* Magazines, was really the *nom de plume* of Hollywood novelist and screenwriter F. Scott Firestone, who died in 1950. Several of his friends have confirmed that Firestone did indeed know a small-time Los Angeles detective and drinking buddy named Dick Danger, who had lifted his nick-name from the popular "Dick Private, Private Dick" comic strip of the time.

"Dr. Firesign's Theatre of the Plains;" a radio operetta, "Twenty Years Behind the Whale;" soap serial "Over The Edge;" the "Hemlock Stones" favorite, "By The Light of the Silvery;"[406] and "A Life in the Day," the last an audio portrait of an average day on American radio circa 1939.

Oz applied for the rights to these and other curious relics of the medium's past and quickly put together a cadre of tie-died associates — actor/Irish tenor Phil Punter, fresh from ABC's *Groovy*, a rip-off of The Monkees, and the L.A. KXLA radio morning team of Austman & Austeen, suddenly hot after a sensationally successful fund-raising marathon.[407]

This quartet, using the venerable "Firesign" brand, first with the founder's name added ("Oz's Firesign") revived many "old" radio shows and produced random and 'pataphysical record albums until both radio and records were seized and sealed by Federal Authorities in 1980. Oz, by then in the music business, created the Firesign Jazz Quartet (Nick, Bob, Dickie and Bud) who were too cool too late.

Meanwhile, Doc, George and Harry, well aware of the strong Firesign traditions they shared, pored over young Ames' archives of

Firesign memorabilia, in search of a clue to the answer of the Zen Bum-like question, "What is Reality?" They found It in one of Doc's former clients, Hideo Gump, Jr.

Hideo, largely unknown to Western audiences, had been the premier "Lock & Load" star of the East. His songs, like the haunted "Ghost Ticket to America," the driving "Yellow People Blues," and his Rock Sinphoney, "Fast Boy," sold millions worldwide. In 1968, however, at the age of twenty-seven, he was a burnt-out shell due to the intense amount of "Drugs and Liquor" he had consumed. Yet, his frustration and bitterness was destined to make him a star once again, a "Rockin' Tiger," as Ames called him. His return to the screen as the Japanese Franchise's "Young Guy, Motor Detective"[408] gave him back to his adoring public.[409]

---

[406] Hemlock himself turned eighty-five in 1965 and, in a piece for *Country Matters Monthly*, professed a "tremendous appetite for boogie-woogie," but was beyond appearances before the public, having just reached the black-belt level in Sudanese Bee Dancing, a whirling and very private affair.

[407] For part psychedelic, part whacko KPFK which was, before its capture by Maoist gorillas in the mid-70s, a home for some of everything, running time and degree of potential boredom notwithstanding.

[408] Young Guy, Miki and Rotonoto were surprised when a new character was introduced in the second season — Lt. Brad Shaw, played by Rothman in Japanese so poor that audible subtitles were needed to explain his jokes.

[409] Hideo Gump Jr. is the grandson of Marmaduke and Yakama Gump, revered founders of the famous country-music dynasty, the Gump Family. Marmaduke's son, Hideo, a close friend of W. C. Fields, married Arlene Yukamoto of Fresno, California, a war heroine later imprisoned in one of the terrible "Strawberry Camps" of WWII. After the war, the family moved to the Japanese country-music capital of Shenzo, giving the genre a brief boom, especially for banjo players like "Country Joe" and "Nippon Cadet."

*Toyko TV's "Young Guy's" nemesis, "Lt. Brad Shaw"*

During the early 1970s, the group then known by the Japanese equivalent of "Four or Five Crazee Guys" were active in all facets of entertainment, including "Woodstock, Yes Baby!" a twenty-acre replica of a typical American village, with real Indians, bears, Hippies, a "Dwarf Golf Course" and, of course, a "Ranchuru Burrulo" for the kids.[410]

With characteristic business acumen, the English language franchise to the Firesign names was sold by its by-then owner Sony a decade later, not, as one might expect, to "Oz's Firesign" which bombed in Boston and tanked in Philly on the road with backup guitarist Porko Suidai in 1980, but to an outfit of Yale graduates, Hipsters and bunco artists who used the name for a pre-Broadway revue, *Dr. Firesign's Fighting Clones*. Fronted by producer Derek Darling,[411] the show was to feature the talents of Vegas soul men, The Eight Shoes; the imported or 5 Crazee Guys.[412] It opened to mixed reviews.

---

[410] Closed in 1998 several years after the last of the four owners had left the country.

[411] Who was, not surprisingly, George Tirebiter's producing partner in Fleetwood Films back in the late 1940's. His early work was with burlesque star Dixie Cupps.

[412] "*Noir* on opium," opined Times critic Kevin Thomas. "Stupid," said Lilly Tomlinson. "I wish I'd been there," wished Robin Williams.

*"The Oleomargerines" in an appearance before the House Un-Amurkan Activities Committee*

Performances, which included male nudity, landed Pete Casman, Flip Philips, Dr. L.P. and Donny O'steen[413] in trouble as they traveled through the Midwest. For reasons known only to themselves they reformed as a retro "Colored"[414] band, "The Oleomargerines," and worked clubs and public radio marathons before leaving show business for individual careers in the price-fixing and derivatives bundling business.

Tirebiter left Japan after only a few weeks, to establish residence in Glendale, California so that he could run for political office. His scandal-laden run for Vice President on the Nat'l Surrealist ticket in 1976 has been reported elsewhere, along with the rest of his career as writer, teacher and performer. Upon his eighty-eighth birthday in December 2008 he said, "I am now twice infinity in years and pleased to have done everything at least once for myself and once for charity."

---

[413] All were reported to like sports, girls and "just generally kickin' it around."

[414] Not actually colored, but tinted.

**"DR. FIRESIGN'S FIGHTING CLONES"**
*Cover shots for the LP "Mode Sportif," 1980*

Harry Ames retired in 1984, having socked away a fortune with an early "Firesign Guide" book, "The Firesign Guide to Idiots." Doc Rothman stayed on at the buffalo ranch until 1990 when he moved to Beverly Hills to run "Entertainment Tonight" and produce three "Angie" and two "Grungie" Awards before accepting a Lifetime Achievement Prize, which he took with him to a second home in Puerto Rico where he died a typically steamy death.

"Oz" and his onetime partners occasionally return to the stage as the "Original and Entire Firesign Theatre," so keeping the name alive for yet another generation by performing those wonderful old radio scripts he found so long ago in a used book at a jumble sale, including, on occasion, the very play that forms the bulk of this volume, *Anythynge You Want To*.[415]

---

[415] They are reported to be doing so in 2011, even though they are now over 275 years old.

"The Eight Shoes"
Cover shot for 1980 Buttfly LP "Gettin' Too Cool Now!"

# LAST TIMES TONITE!

## THE CELEBRATED QUARTET

# DR. FIRESIGN'S THEATRE
### OF THE PLAINS
IN
## "THE GIANT RAT OF SUMATRA"
PLUS
## "THE COUNT OF MONTE CRISTO"

# "The Count of Monte Cristo"

As performed circa 1900 by Dr. Firesign's Theatre
Of The Plains and Buffalo Show
From a Partial Script found in the Zachariah Collection,
Solid State University

**Dr. F:** Ladies and gentlemen, good evening. The assembled company is proud to present their widely acclaimed historical tragedy in five acts, "Waiting For the Count of Monte Cristo, or Someone Like Him." Our justly famous Opium Balls and Opium Balm will be on sale during the four intermissions. After the play, ladies are welcome in the dressing room to meet the cast. But now, let the play begin!

**(FANFARE)**

### DUC DE CODGER
A wonderful dinner, but alas, Friar Beepo,
my final hour draws nigh and still no word
of my dear nephew, that bastard, Edmond.

### BEEPO
Don't exert yourself needlessly, your Lordship,
over the likes of him.

**(SOUNDS OF A SWORDFIGHT OFFSTAGE)**

### DANTES
(ENTERING): Your niece, my cousin, refused
me entrance to your rooms, sir. Is it true that
you are ailing? So am I.

### DUC
We'll talk of that later, my boy.

### DANTES
Thanks. Goodbye.

**DUC**
But now, before I am to slip into the sleep of sleeps, I needs must reveal to you a great and aweful secret.

**DANTES**
Oh, Nuncle, Nuncle, speak not of sleeping.

**DUC**
Nay, I am for't. But fear you not. Come, bend over. You, Edmond Dantes are not the foundling that you think, but the only son and true and rightful heir to the weighty fortunes of the Count of . . . aaaagggahhh. (DIES)

**DANTES**
I don't know any Count of Argh. I know of Duke of Earghh.

**BEEPO**
(COVERING BODY): He's dead. Oh, piteous time. I'll bear these tidings to the king.

**DANTES**
(KNEELING): Oh, mercenary destiny, that marbles up the sweetened tooth of time with black disguise. I'll fill my bucket silly with revenge, till blood shall douche the anger from mine eyes.

**UNCLE**
(ENTERING) Nephew?

**DANTES**
Gezeundheit!

**UNCLE**
Your couplet runneth over. Come, in this hour of mutual greed, let us share a flagon of churning burgundy. (ASIDE) And now my action's clear. And now I'll do't. This foundling cur was known to be my brother's favorite, and thus is bound to find some favor in his will. And so, to flavor my good fortunes, I'll pack him off to Heaven to be my

brother's keeper, and thus to keep the better's best myself. Eddie my love! (OFFERING GOBLET) Here's drink for you.

**DANTES**
(RAISING HIS OWN GOBLET) And drink for you!

**(THEY LINK ARMS AND DRINK FROM THEIR OWN GOBLETS)**

**UNCLE**
(ASIDE) It won't be long . . e'en now the venom surges to his brain . . . death's knocking at his door and yet he smiles . . . He'll drop like a stone

**. . . (UNCLE DOES AND DIES)**

**DANTES**
What? Dead again? Where are his smiles — his curdling mirth? They've left me groatless to seek the secret of my secret birth. I'll take some speed and beat the Queen to Perth.

**MARIE**
(ENTERING): Oh, no, you're not.

**DANTES**
Ah, my fiancée, Cousine Marie. Quel surprise!

**MARIE**
No, no. Oui, oui, I'm not.

**DANTES**
What? What say you, saucy wrench?

**MARIE**
Unbeknownst to you, I am your twin brother Edmund, Edmund.

DANTES
Is't true? But Marie, my love, then we can never be married.

MARIE
And you shall never live to inherit my father's fortune.

DANTES
Why should I take a woman's word for that?

MARIE
'Nuff said. Take this instead.
(HE PULLS OUT HIS MANLY SWORD
AND BRANDISHES IT) And this and this
and that. On garde, you swine!

DANTES
I'll guard my swine 'til death do part us both.
(LUNGING) Have at you!

MARIE
Gazuntheit!

**(THEY FIGHT. MARIE DIES. HIS BONNET AND PIGTAILS FALL OFF. HIS MANLY SWORD STICKS UPRIGHT.)**

DANTES
He's gone and still she acts.

DUC
(SITTING UP): Well fought, my son.

DANTES
My Nuncle's ghost!

DUC
Not your Nuncle, but your Dad!

DANTES
My father's ghost?

DUC
Not a ghost neither.

DANTES
Not my father?

**DUC**
Yes, my son. And I have proof!
Read what is writ upon your dagger's dirk,
the twin to mine.

**DANTES**
This dagger dirk? T'was given me at birth.

**DUC**
The very same.

**DANTES**
(READING): "I am he of whom he speaks." That's proof enough for me.

**DUC**
And so we seal our secret kinship with a kiss.

**DANTES**
Son!

**DUC**
Father!

**BOTH**
My son!

**(DANTES RUNS TO EMBRACE THE DUC AND IMPALES HIMSELF UPON THE KNIFE.)**

**DANTES**
Alas, I'm hurt! There's nothing more to say. And no one's left to write an ending to this dismal play.

**(DANTES DIES. THE DUC THEN PUTS ON MARIE'S BONNET AND PIGTAILS.)**

**DUC**
Now I can marry the Count!

**(HE EXITS.)**

## APACHE BUFFALO BALANCING ACT FOLLOWS

"And now you gwine pay yo' carpet tax!"
"ORPHAN'S TEARS"
A Bowman & Archer Production for Mixville Pictures (1912)

# "ORPHAN'S TEARS
## or, Buckboard Virtue Rewarded"

A 19th Century Melodrama Performed by
Dr. Firesign's Theatre of the Plains

### Act One

*The Drawing Room of Belleweather, the lavish plantation home of the Cowards. Now fallen on hard times, BAUREGARD is drawing as BEULABELLE runs in:*

**BELLE:** Beauregard! Beauregard Coward!

**BEAU:** What is it, my darling sister?

**BELLE:** Oh, wonderful news! The War is over! The brutal, industrial North has been defeated by the gentlemanly, agricultural South! Our Daddy's comin' home!

**DADDY:** (ENTERING FROM THE CELLAR) Ah never left, Butterbelle! No true Mississippi Coward would leave his Plantation, his wine cellar and the virtue of his women undefended in such a dangerous time. Hello, son.

**BEAU:** Why, Father! I thought you were a Colonel!

**DADDY:** Ah am! A Colonel — and a Coward! And I shall live to be a General!

**BELLE:** Oh, Daddy! What a happy day! We've won! And you — already a General. Think of the balls we'll have!

**BEAU:** You're too young to think about that, Beulaballs — er — bells. Think instead of cannon balls. Think of the brothers we've lost! And, I'd be with them now, but for this cursed wound!

**DADDY:** Yes, my poor son — who shares with me the hereditary Coward war wound — a toe blown off at birth.

**BELLE:** Just another tragic consequence of this foolish War, Father. With all the Colored folks on the front lines, there's nobody left to hold positions of responsibility in the cotton fields and in the banks.

**DADDY:** Right, son! If our old, faithful Uncle Tom Quadroon were in the White House now, instead of that man, Johnson . .

**BEAU:** They should impeach that War Criminal!

**DADDY:** . . . and Old Aunt Vagina were behind the bar instead of Bolinball — er — Beulabelle — we could get down to some serious drinkin' and sober politics!

**BEAU:** And race old Doo-Dah at the Camptown Field, all the live-long day!

**BELLE:** (SINGS) Gwine to rut all night!
Gwine to drink all day!
Drink Wild Turkey 'til my bird falls down,
And they carry me away!

*There is a fearful knocking at the door, a cannon shot rings out! The door crashes inward and UNCLE TOM enters.*

**BELLE:** Why, Uncle Tom! You're back!

**TOM:** Uncle Field Marshal Thomas LaGree Quadroon, honey! Ah'm back, and Ah'm beautiful!

**BEAU:** I'm so glad you're back, Tom! We've missed you here at Bellebottom. The cotton needs chopping, the mule won't start, and my checkbook is seriously out of balance.

**DADDY:** Good to have the slaves back, Tom. (CONFIDENTIALLY) I'd like your honest opinion on buying into Clownstock — 1865 Preferred Debentures . . .

**BELLE:** Oh, Uncle Tom, I haven't been nursed in years!

BEAU: Did you learn any new songs up in Detroit?

TOM: (LAUGHS) Ho! Ho! Ho! Ho! (ANOTHER CANNON SHOT) Dis is no laffin' mattah!

DADDY: That's right, Tom. I forgot. You're a Free Man now!

TOM: Oh, no Ah ain't! Ah's expensive! Ah's a Pro-fessional Slave now! You been walkin' ovah dis kinky ol' carpet fo' sixty year . . .

BELLE: Has it really been that long, Uncle Tom?

TOM: . . . An' now you gwine pay yo' Carpet Tax! Put it right here — in de bag! (INDICATES CARPET BAG)

DADDY: Blasphemy! I'll die first. (HE FALLS OVER DEAD)

BELLE: He's dead!

TOM: It's a New World now, honey! Nobody's gwine hab to be a Slave all the time no mo'! We's gwine take turns! And guess whose turn it is now!

*The Orphan Cowards cower, as Uncle Tom menaces them with a bullwhip.*

*The Curtain Falls.*

*Reporter Harry Cox (r) with Hawaiian shirt and
Lem Ashauler, Editor of the Hellmouth (CA) newspaper (l)
on the hunt for the aliens who live among us!*

# EVERYTHING YOU KNOW IS WRONG!® ABOUT... "ANYTHYNGE YOU WANT TO"®

*Authors' Note: The Firesign's unexpurgated first-draft script for the "Everything" LP released in 1975 was written in June 1974. It revealed yet another story about Dr. Firesign and his show-business partners as told by Harry Cox, then President of the Funny Names Clubs of America. Cox had worked as cinematographer with Firesign in 1927, shooting "The White Buffalo" on location in Bat City, Mexico. The movie itself recounted a psychedelic scene set in Curio, Arizona around 1900, following a performance of the first act of "Orphan's Tears." This draft was never fully recorded.*

**COX:** I don't know how you came by this record, but you are now embarked upon a journey that must certainly lead you to change your life forever. If you were never a "special person," you are a Special Person now.

I'm in Cabin #3 of the Lonely Mice Motel in Hellmouth, California. This is midway between the Border and the point marked "B" on the map. You don't need to know how I've come this far. It's a miracle. A strange place for a successful lumber executive with a loving family to spend his 75th birthday — alone — the heat — it's terrible! I don't know how much more time I have. In fact, I don't know how much more time any of us have on this planet. The signs are everywhere! The Sacred Symbols of Mu on the front page of today's Hellmouth Heater-Democrat! Listen — if I turned on the radio right now . . . (MOVING OFF) . . . but — you wouldn't understand. Not yet. I've got to start long ago, in the middle, where I came in.

**(RATTLE OF NOTES)**

My name is Harold B. (for "Bigfoot") Cox, of Sasquatch, Washington State. Back at that time — 1925 — I was a cameraman, working on the Bowman & Archer lot down in Southern California.

I was a young man then, but I'd done a half-dozen epics for the studio, so they asked me to go down to Bat City, Mexico, to do "The White Buffalo" — which was going to be the biggest location picture since I shot the Dish Sisters in "Buckboard Virtue."

**(LOCTION SOUNDS UNDER)**

Everything had been going wrong that day, and it was so hot we had to stand in each other's shadows for relief. Archer was directing and our star, Lila Lomond, who was having one of her daily attacks . . .

**LILA:** (SOBBING) Mr. Bowman! You're the Producer — you have to do something! How do you expect me to act in this heat? I'm so hot my legs are sticking together! I can't even remember my lines! . . .

**BOWMAN:** It's a silent film for crissake! Look, Archer, try another take — we're behind schedule. We gotta burn the field today.

**ARCHER:** Right you are, Abe. Alright, Lily, honey. Let's just try to take another one while the buffalo's quiet, please, sweetheart. Alright, Harry — you got enough film for another take?

**COX:** Oh, sure, Mr. Archer. The camera jammed on the last one, so we still have half a load. Crank froze up in the heat . . .

**LILA:** I'm not surprised! Poor Frank! Everybody throws up in this heat! I'm going to throw up now!

**BOWMAN:** Don't throw up, not on your costume! We've got close ups to do.

**ARCHER:** Let's just try it once more before we lose the light. You ready, Rex?

**REX:** My torch has gone out!

| | |
|---|---|
| ARCHER: | Leo? Where's Leo? |
| COX: | He's checking the camera towers for the big burn-off. |
| ARCHER: | That's right. Light it yourself, Rex! |
| REX: | Yes! I'll light it! Ha! I'll hold it up to the sun! |
| LILA: | Oh, Rex! |
| REX: | I'll light it with my contract! |
| ARCHER: | OK, kids! Let's be professionals, please. It's almost 4 o'clock. Let's just do it. Roll 'em, Cox. |
| COX: | Cranking! |
| CAMERA ASST: | Cranking at speed, Mr. Cox. |
| ARCHER: | Light that torch, Rex! You'll start the buffalo moving. Not so fast. All right, Lila, honey. Remember now, the buffalo is the only thing left from the old plantation. Touch the buffalo — don't flinch! Don't flinch! Good! Good, good! |
| BOWMAN: | Good, good! Dynamite! |
| ARCHER: | You getting this, Cox? |
| COX: | Frame by frame. |
| ASST: | 75 feet — 70 feet . . . |
| ARCHER: | Now, you are the buffalo looking out into the fields. Think of the old plantation — beautiful Belleweather — the moss hanging from the old fourposter. Remember everything you've lost. Sigh! |
| LILA: | I'm hot! |
| ARCHER: | No! . . . |
| BOWMAN: | You're not hot, you're miserable! |

| | |
|---|---|
| **LILA:** | I'm hot *and* miserable! |
| **BOWMAN:** | Right! Remember — you and your brother, sold into slavery to Mexican bandits, south of the border. Think of Beauregard, helpless, forced to toil in the deadly hemp fields with the Indians. And you, Beulabelle, condemned to marry a man whose face you've never seen! |
| **ARCHER:** | Keep your hand on the buffalo, dear. Stroke him. Stroke his hump. Beauregard! Rex! Action. |
| **COX:** | I've got Beauregard in frame. |
| **BOWMAN:** | What's happening now? |
| **LILA:** | I'm hot! |
| **BOWMAN:** | Yes, but no! Here comes your brother across the field! What's that in his hand? That's right! It's a torch. He's running towards you . . . |
| **ARCHER:** | Don't trip, don't trip! . . . Get up! |
| **BOWMAN AND OTHERS:** | Get up! |
| **ARCHER:** | Keep running, it looks great! (TO COX) Did you get that? |
| **COX:** | Yeah — (LAUGHS) — sure . . . |
| **BOWMAN:** | Now you're shocked, Lila! What has he done? |
| **ARCHER:** | Bauregard! Shout to her! |
| **REX:** | The fields are burning! |
| **BOWMAN AND OTHERS:** | Good! That's great! |
| **COX:** | I'm getting it! |
| **ASST:** | Twenty feet, Mr. Cox. |
| **REX:** | No, you don't understand! The fields are burning! |
| **BOWMAN:** | Terrific! |

| | |
|---|---|
| **LILA:** | I smell smoke! |
| **COX:** | Smells like a Hollywood party. |
| **BOWMAN:** | Jeezus H. Christ! They've already set the stuff on fire! Leo! Where the hell's Leo? |
| **ARCHER:** | Cut! Cut! Cox, you better get up a tower and get one of the cameras rolling! Leo, what's going on? |
| **LEO:** | Mr. Archer! Mr. Bowman! Someone has set the fields afire too soon! All the camera towers are burning! |
| **BOWMAN:** | Let's get out of here! That stuff's burning like toilet paper! |
| **ARCHER:** | Leo, release the Extras! Get the animals out of here! Cox, are you still rolling? |
| **COX:** | I'm out of film! |
| **LEO:** | Arriba los Extrros! Innundados los penos the animales! |

**GENERAL COMMOTION FADING UNDER**

| | |
|---|---|
| **COX:** | (NARRATING) It was terrible! A complete disaster! That hemp farm was so big it was still on fire at four in the morning, when Leo Artunian — overcome by smoke — asked me to help him back to our headquarters — which were in the ancient Indian ruins they called "Batsitlan." "Bat City" we called it, but since then I've learned its Other Name. You will too, soon enough! Well, I'd never gotten too close to this Artunian. He was a foreigner — a drifter. Like most white men in the Mexican desert. But he seemed a pleasant enough fellow. Bowman and Archer had taken a particular fancy to him — made him Location Director, then Production Manager. But — it looked like we were both out of work now, so I thought I'd let him buy me a drink in the local cantina . . . |

**CROSSFADE TO NIGHT LOCATION**

| | |
|---|---|
| **COX:** | Are you feeling all right, Leo? How about a drink? |
| **LEO:** | (COUGHING) OK, but let's sit outside. My head is still reeling from the smoke. (TO WAITER) Hola, Pio! Dos Mayans! |

**PIO:** Si, senor! Dos Mayans, con huevos, por los gringos!

**LEO:** Let's sit over there by the old wall.

**COX:** Well, they're all old, Leo. Just sit down right here . . .

**LEO:** No, no. From this one here you can see the rising moon part the Idol's conk.

**COX:** That thing gives me the shivers! It must be 50 feet high.

**LEO:** It was much higher than that, before the missionaries toppled the mirror beacon.

**COX:** The what?

**LEO:** Wig hat — er — ceremonial headdress. It was beautiful.

**COX:** How do you know that?

**LEO:** How does anyone know? Legends, rumors, tales, suppositories — er — supposed stories of the Great and Hidden Past.

**COX:** Still looks like a bat with a gas mask to me.

**PIO:** Sus cervezas, senores.

**COX:** Gracias! (DRINKS) This Mayan Beer tastes like urine.

**LEO:** It's in the water.

**DOOR OPENS AND CLOSES ON CANTINA, FOOTSTEPS, UNDER**

**BOWMAN:** . . . It's little Lila I'm worried about. The other's 'll float. They'll get work. Little Lila'll have to do dog pictures after this. Think of her folks. It'll kill 'em.

**ARCHER:** Think of the dogs. 'Scuse me. I've gotta drain the monster.

**BOWMAN:** You do that while I talk to the stones. Ladies and gentlemen! Chickens, drunks, idols — and my dear cinemaphotographer and production director! Although the press has not arrived, let me announce to you and me and all the Mezzo-Americans herewith assembled that "The White Buffalo" has stumbled and fallen, never to get up, again. The shooting's over, boys. We're all washed up.

ARCHER: I told you — this place is a hex, Bowman.

BOWMAN: Hex marks the spot. Bad luck for buffalos. Always has been, remember?

LEO: Excuse me, gentlemen. Are you referring to your previous enterprise in this area? You know, the Bowman-Archer treasure hunt of 1900?

ARCHER: There, Abe! I'm right! I told you he knows more than he should. Either that or you told him.

BOWMAN: I wouldn't tell him — not about that.

LEO: Of course! How could I have known? There was only the two of you and the buffalo.

ARCHER: You told him!

BOWMAN: Come on, Marsh! I never told anybody!

LEO: They wouldn't have believed you anyway. But I believe you. I was there. I was the buffalo!

## REACTION LINES UNDER

COX: (NARRATING) Sound strange? Men turning into buffalos? Buffalos turning into men? This was only part of the world that was revealed to me in the bizarre story the three of them unfolded. It seems that at the turn of the century, Abe Bowman and Marshall Archer were touring the Great Southwest with an old-time Medicine Show. They made their pitch after entertaining the marks with that old chestnut of the plains — "Orphan's Tears."

*Here might be interpolated the extant script for Act One of "Orphan's Tears," reproduced elsewhere in this volume. The "Everything You Know Is Wrong" manuscript continues like this:*

**ARCHER:** Thank you! Thank you, boys, for your enthusiastic enjoyment for Act One of "Orphan's Tears!" While the lovely Beaulabelle slips out of her tights and into her Mayan slave costume for the wicked and sensual second act, here's dramatic news from my partner, the eminent Professor "Honest Abraham" Bowman, late of the Missouri Valley Seminole Sexuary!

**BOWMAN:** Thank you, Dr. Archer! Now, I want every man, woman, child, Indian or Mexican to reach into his britches and pull out a one dollar bill. Look at it. On one side, the picture of a dead man — a former president and a rope smoker! On the other side, a pyramid with an eye on top and some foreign gibberish. Worthless! Except for what you can buy with it here! Yes, that piece of paper, not worth the hemp it's printed on, is good in trade for each of the fine products my partner, the Honorable Professor Marshall Archer, electro-chemist and phrenologist and corresponding graduate of Dr. Bedowe's Pneumatic Institute of Witchcraft, Mass., is displaying before your startled gaze.

**ARCHER:** Yes, ladies and gentlemen, chickens and Mexicans — hidden inside this curious tin is a paste with the power of fire within. A secret Egyptian formula transmitted from beyond the grave to the famous dead Indian hero, Chief Dancing Knockout. Yes, Chief Knockout's Pyramid Pushover Paste! Good for chilblains, high livers, female distress and release of nightwater!

**SHERIFF:** I'll take one!

**BOWMAN:** One is not enough, Sheriff Axehandle! No sirree! All the power of the pyramids isn't worth a Hindoo monkey if you can't go to sleep afterwards! Yes, if you suffer from bed sticking, guilt tremors or common rump itch — if a wolf, a gunshot, the slightest thing will keep you awake — well, pardner, you can sleep tight without fright! Drink Swami Ganja's Nightmare Moon Juice in your bunk tonight!

**VOICE OF MAYOR:** I'll take two!

**ARCHER:** Thank you, Mayor Asshanger! But still, it's not enough! Yes, it takes three to make a sale! Friends, do you have shoulders like a Roughrider, but a voice like a prairie hen? Are you the victim of miner's lung, alkali throat or dusty veins? All can be

**"Don Bruhaha's Inca Hell Oil Tonic**

instantly combated by the simple internal application of Don Brujaja's Inca Hell Oil Tonic! 95 percent pure cactus alcohol, 5 percent Mexican serpent syrup. Not a narcotic — it's the real thing!

**DEPUTY:** How do we know they work?

**BOWMAN:** An intelligent question, Deputy Buttwhumper. You know they work because every package, vial, flask, philaster or pill pot is personally packaged and perfectly sealed under the hermetic supervision of Dr. Elmo Firesign, at his extensive pharmaceutical offices in Animal, Missouri.

**ARCHER:** Yes, the Pushover Paste, the Moon Juice and the Hell Oil Tonic! Our 19th century price was a dollar apiece . . .

**VOICE:** Too much!

**ARCHER:** But in this brand-new century — 3-for-a-dollar, including the price of admission to Act Two of "Orphan's Tears," which is just about to start inside the tent.

**VOICES:** Come on, boys! Let's buy some!

**SHERIFF:** Hold it! Is it safe?

**BOWMAN:** Safe as buffalo milk, Sheriff. And to prove it, Professor Archer is preparing a potation for our personal libation! One part Paste, one Part Juice and just a potent jot of Hell Oil! Thank you Archer. Yes, we'll drink it before your very eyes! Here's a toast to the brave and bully boys of the Arizona Territory!

**AUDIENCE RESPONSE, FADING UNDER**

**COX:** (NARRATING) How could they have known? Had the ubiquitous Dr. Firesign mixed up a bad batch, or did Archer drop in an extra jigger of Moon Juice? Or — something stranger? I have my theories, but we'll never know. What they told me was, that Bowman had no sooner lowered his glass, than he witnessed the sudden transformation of Marshall Archer into a silver crow. And Archer simultaneously observed the similar metamorphosis of his partner Abe. Large, silver crows. Four foot high — and one of 'em with glasses. Each lifted his wings in surprise and rose like a shot, leaving the town of Curio, Arizona and its bewildered populace 500 feet below — a silent speck on the vast Western desert floor.

**WING AND FLYING EFFECT UNDER**

**COX:** Unable to speak to one another, but pursuing the same course, they soared like brothers all that day, and perhaps another, floating on each other's thoughts, never moving their wings, yet journeying a great distance to the South.

**BOWMAN AND ARCHER CROW-THOUGHT UNDER:** Feel the sun on my back . . . the pink mountains . . . A good looking crow against the sun . . .

**ARCHER/CROW:** Smell the water . . .

**BOWMAN/CROW:** Dive . . .

**ARCHER/CROW:** A river of buffalo drinking from a hidden spring . . .

**BOWMAN/CROW:** In their midst, a white buffalo . . .

| | |
|---|---|
| COX: | (NARRATING) Balanced on a raft of water in an endless river of reeds, they conversed inexplicably with an ancient cockroach in a sombrero they knew instantly to be . . . |
| DON B: | Don Brujaja. Ha ha ha ha! Follow the snake. Follow the snake. The snake is a river . . . (HE RATTLES AND LAUGHS) |
| BOWMAN/CROW: | Rattle and laugh . . . |
| COX: | And they jumped on his back . . . |
| DON B: | Jump on my back . . . |
| COX: | . . . and rode it hard like a bronco . . . |
| DON B: | Ride me to the sea . . . |
| COX: | . . . to where the snake was swallowed by the sea. And they looked in a direction they had never looked before . . . |
| DON B: | (LAUGHING) Look! Look! |
| COX: | . . . and they saw a City of gold and amber and crystal . . . |
| DON B: | Gold! . . . Crystal . . . |
| COX: | . . . in the sky at the bottom of the sea. And at the gate of that city . . . |
| DON B: | Gate . . . |
| COX: | . . . a white buffalo was grazing . . . |
| DON B: | White buffalo . . . |
| COX: | . . . and raising its great head . . . |
| DON B: | LAUGHTER, FADING |
| COX: | . . . met their gaze directly . . . |

*Sadly, the conclusion of the White Buffalo story is nowhere to be found. Harry Cox was interrupted at this point in his recording by a phonecall from Nino The Mindbender that derailed poor Cox's narrative entirely, in favor of a story about Aliens having landed and impregnated his neighbors, the Crumbhungers, subjects of a television travel show, "The Golden Hind." Just proves the old saying, "Everything You Know Is Wrong!*

# "THE ARMENIAN'S PAW, or BUFFALO CHIPS WON'T YOU COME OUT TONIGHT, or, THE ARMENIAN'S PAW, or NONE OF THE ABOVE"

### A Tale of Dr. Firesign's Theatre of the Plains As Told By The Firesign Theatre

### THE CAST
*Harry, Boy, Old Man* — Phil Austin
*Dr. Firesign* — Peter Bergman
*Archer, The Announcer* — David Ossman
*Leo, Artunian, Lama* — Phil Proctor

*As presented at The Magic Mushroom,*
*December 17, 1967*

**MUSIC CUE IN:**

**ANNOUNCER:** The Firesign Theatre Presents: The Armenian's Paw, or Buffalo Chips Won't You Come Out Tonight, or, The Armenian's Paw, or None of the Above . . .

**MUSIC UP AND OUT**

**ANN:** The Scene: The faded grandeur of the Teatro Burrito Grande Theater in downtown Guacamole, Chile . . .

**VOICE:** And I'll have the number three dinner, please, dear.

**ANN:** . . . Where at this very moment, in the flickering lime-light of the gas-lit stage . . .

**OTHER VOICE:** Hold the refried beans on mine, please.

*"mrmrmrmrmr" Phil Proctor as Art, the Buffalo.*
**THE FIRESIGN THEATRE AT**
**THE MAGIC MUSHROOM, 1967**

ANN: ... Dr. Firesign's Original Traveling Antique Theatre of the Plains and Buffalo Show is concluding the 8,412 continuous performance of its immortal favorite ... Waiting For The Count of Monte Cristo, or Someone Like Him.

**CROSS TO THEATRE**

ARCHER: ... And so you, Edmond Dantes, are the true Count of Monte Cristo!

HARRY: I am?

ARCHER: No, you're not!

DR FIRESIGN: Because I am!

HARRY: But that's impossible!

| | |
|---|---|
| **LEO:** | How's that? |
| **DR. F:** | Fine, thanks. How's this? |
| **LEO:** | Not bad. |
| **ARCHER:** | Not good! |
| **HARRY:** | Why not? |
| **LEO:** | Because you are my sister! |
| **DR. F:** | Then we can never be married! |
| **ARCHER:** | I knew it all along. |
| **HARRY:** | But we are married! |
| **LEO:** | So are we! |
| **HARRY:** | Thank god! (DIES) |
| **ARCHER:** | Our friend the Count of Monte Cristo's dead. And so, with saddened heart and lowered head, let's leave the dead in peace. Gentlemen, the feast. |

## THE CURTAIN FALLS

| | |
|---|---|
| **DR. F:** | Ladies and gentlemen! With your kind indulgence, please! Our performance tonight will conclude — as advertised — with Dr. Firesign's world-reknowned Buffalo Tableau in Three Scenes . . . |

## VOICES: WHISTLES AND APPLAUSE

| | |
|---|---|
| **HARRY:** | The buffalo's sick, Doctor. |
| **DR. F:** | Well, the buffalo must go on! |
| **HARRY:** | But he just threw up all over my trunk! |
| **DR. F:** | I don't care. |
| **HARRY:** | I do! It's my trunk! |

| | |
|---|---|
| **DR. F:** | Well, it's my buffalo! And he's on! |

**DRUMROLL AND CURTAIN OPENS**

| | |
|---|---|
| **DR. F:** | Tableau One! "The American Buffalo At Play!" |

**TABLEAU AND CURTAIN**

| | |
|---|---|
| **DR. F:** | Tableau Two! "The American Buffalo Pursued By An American Indian!" |

**TABLEAU AND CURTAIN**

| | |
|---|---|
| **DR. F:** | Tableau Three! "The Death of the American Buffalo!" |

**TABLEAU AND CURTAIN FOLLOWED BY OMINOUS GRUMBLING**

| | |
|---|---|
| **DR. F:** | Let's get out of here, boys! |
| **ARCHER:** | Don't forget the buffalo! |
| **DR F:** | I wish I could! |
| **HARRY:** | Run for your lives . . . |

**DOOR SLAM FOLLOWED BY HEAVY BREATHING**

| | |
|---|---|
| **DR. F:** | Lock the door. All right, are we all here? |
| **LEO:** | Where's the buffalo? |
| **HARRY:** | He's in the bathroom. |
| **DR. F:** | Go hold his head, Harry. |
| **HARRY:** | All right. |
| **DR. F:** | Leo, start packing! Now that the buffalo's gone, we can talk. |
| **LEO:** | I sure hope they don't find out which hotel we're staying at. |

**KNOCK KNOCK**

| | |
|---|---|
| **ARCHER:** | It's too late! The same thing happened to me once in Springfield . . . |
| **DR. F:** | Shhhh! Get the door, Leo. |

**DOOR OPENS**

| | |
|---|---|
| **BOY:** | Is this the Firestone Antique Theater? |
| **DR. F:** | They just left. |
| **BOY:** | Oh, that's too bad. I got a telegram for them. |
| **ARCHER:** | Well, boy, they left their buffalo. You can give it to him. |
| **ART:** | mrmrmrmrmrmr |
| **BOY:** | Hey! That's a pretty nice buffalo for a '58, man. It's been lowered, huh? All right, stand back. You going to get a singing telegram!<br>  How are things in Guacamole?<br>  Is my little troupe still playing there?<br>  'Cause if they run you out of town,<br>  Don't wear a frown!<br>  You're booked in Yucatan!<br>  Bat City. Two weeks. Lots a luck.<br>Signed, your agent, Buffalo Billy Morris. P. S. Is the buffalo feeling any better? OK, you got a reply? |
| **ART:** | mrmrmrmrmrmr |
| **BOY:** | How do you spell that? |
| **DR. F:** | With a double mrmr! Get out! |

**DOOR SLAMS**

| | |
|---|---|
| **ARCHER:** | Bat City, Yucatan! It's the end! |
| **LEO:** | What's the matter with Bat City? |
| **DR F:** | Bat City, my boy, is Act Six. |
| **ARCHER:** | It's like playing for your parents. |

| | |
|---|---|
| **LEO:** | But if we open in Bat City . . . |
| **HARRY:** | Nobody opens in Bat City. It's always closing night. |
| **DR F:** | Well, gentlemen — what could we expect in an age when no one appreciates Art? |
| **ART:** | mrmrmrmrmrmr |
| **DR F:** | Quiet, Art! We're all in this together. Everybody put on a disguise, and we'll go out and have a drink at the Cantina. |

**TRANSITION SOUNDS — CAR HORNS, SPANISH VOICES**

| | |
|---|---|
| **LEO:** | Well, maybe we could quit show business instead of playing Bat City. |
| **ARCHER:** | It's the same thing, boy. |
| **HARRY:** | There must be another town we can play. |
| **LEO:** | We've run out of towns. |
| **DR F:** | No, we've been run out of towns. |
| **ARCHER:** | It's the same thing. |
| **HARRY:** | Where's the Cantina? I'm thirsty. |
| **ARCHER:** | It's on the corner. |
| **HARRY:** | When are they going to put it in a building? |
| **LEO:** | Where did Art go? |
| **DR. F:** | He just shuffled into that little gift shop. He must be hunting for a souvenir. |
| **ARCHER:** | Well, quick, get him! He hasn't any money! |
| **HARRY:** | He has a couple of human nickels. |
| **DR F:** | Follow him! |

## DING DING DINGLE DING

**ARTUNIAN:** Good evening, gentlemen. Welcome to Artunian's Lamentable Antique Store and Curio Hut.

**HARRY:** Excuse me, but we're looking for a buffalo.

**ARTUNIAN:** Curios you should mention that. The Shah of Persia only yesterday personally gave me this most exquisite beast. Totally hand-encrusted with precious wool. As you can tell, it's been lowered. For a '58, it's a very clean machine. Would you like me to wrap it, or will you eat it here?

**HARRY:** Art! Art, it's you!

**DR F:** Take that hastily scrawled price-tag off his horns!

**ARCHER:** You ought to be ashamed of yourself, Mr. Artunian.

**ARTUNIAN:** Yes, I should. Why don't you putter around the shop while I put on my hair shirt. Be sure and look for the cleverly hidden Maps of various Lost Cities. And feel free to break some ashtrays, I need the money.

**HARRY:** Gee, what as strange man. Did you notice that when he put his right hand in his pocket — he didn't?

**LEO:** I wonder how he lost his hand?

**ARCHER:** Look, boys! Fifty Dollars for a rare Egyptian Death's-head Moth in quartz.

**DR F:** That's a bit much. I wonder if he has it in pints. But wait! Look! Over here. Do you see what I see, vaguely outlined through this imitation milk-glass copy of an Assyrian Middle Kingdom feance Toby Jug?

**ALL:** No!

**DR F:** Well, look closer. It's what appears to be a carefully rolled ancient map-sized papyrus. Is the Armenian still in the back.

**HARRY:** I can't see hide nor hair shirt of him.

| | |
|---|---|
| **LEO:** | I'm back here. |
| **DR F:** | Then cover me. |
| **ALL:** | OK! |
| **ART:** | mrmrmrmrmr |
| **DR F:** | No, boys! Get that buffalo off! Now see what you've done! My hand is caught inside the jug! |
| **ARTUNIAN:** | Well! Surprise, surprise! Your hand seems to be trapped inside my priceless Assyrian Toby Jug. |
| **DR F:** | Why, so it is! |
| **ARTUNIAN:** | Your hand is more important than any priceless jug. You see, I who have only one hand know the value of hands. Go ahead, smash it! |
| **DR F:** | That's awfully good of you, Artunian. |
| **LOUD CRASH** | |
| **ARTUNIAN:** | Ah! You're free — and you owe me twenty dollars. |
| **DR F:** | The money is of no importance. Take a look at this papyrus I found. |
| **ARTUNIAN:** | The papyrus? |
| **DR F:** | Let me see . . . Aha! It's an ancient Assyrian . . . price tag for twenty dollars! |
| **ARTUNIAN:** | Ah, how equitable. |
| **HARRY:** | Look, Dr. Firesign! On the back of the price tag is a . . . |
| **DR F:** | Why, isn't it a . . . |
| **LEO:** | Yes, it is! |
| **HARRY:** | No it isn't. It's an authentic map of a fabled lost city, surely |

|            | filled with valuable relics and the elixir of eternal youth. Let's go find it! |
|---|---|
| **ARTUNIAN:** | Drat! I've been looking for that for years! To have been outwitted in this way by simple tourists! Ooooooo! |
| **DR F:** | Sorry, old man. You'll have to make the best of a bad bargain. |
| **HARRY:** | While we make the best of this map. Can you decipher these strange occult symbols, Mr. Archer? |
| **ARCHER:** | Of course. Let me look. Mmmm . . . three Birds flying East, a Snake eating its tail, and a Jaguar — in the shop. Well, it seems pretty ordinary. What do you make of it, Mr. Artunian? |
| **ARTUNIAN:** | Nothing but profit. Let me look it up in Artunian's Automotive Guide to Fabled Lost Cities. Ah! Here it is. You, my fortunate friends, have stumbled onto the map to the Royal Inca Citadel of Axl Taxl! Lost for thousands of years! You see? Three Birds flying East — enormous treasure! A Snake eating its tail — danger to the unclean! And the sacred Jaguar — camping facilities, chemical toilets and easy access to the Pan American Highway. Would you like me to book you on the next bus? |
| **HARRY:** | Any place is better than Bat City! On to Axl Taxl. Say, what does that mean, anyway? |
| **ARTUNIAN:** | Axl Taxl? Roughly translated — Bat City. |
| **DR F:** | Come on, boys. I'll pay for the Toby Jug. Here, you Tasmanian devil! |
| **ARTUNIAN:** | Keep your tongue, or I'll give you the back of my hand! |
| **DR F:** | We'll take it! |
| **ARTUNIAN:** | You want my hand? Why? |
| **DR F:** | Because of that curious lavender spot just beneath your knuckle. |

| | |
|---|---|
| ARTUNIAN: | Why, that's nothing but a birthmark my mother gave to me. |
| ARCHER: | But, Dr. Firesign — we can't afford . . . |
| DR F: | Quiet, old man! I've traveled this wide world over, ten thousand miles or more, but an authentic map of the fabled Lost City of Shangra Deelite on the back of an Armenian shopkeeper's hand, I never done seen before. |
| ARCHER: | Shangra Deelite! |
| ALL: | My God! Etc. |
| DR F: | Mr. Artunian, we want to buy your hand. |
| ARTUNIAN: | My hand? My one remaining hand? This dear hand? Why all the perfumes in Arabia could not buy it! If you tickle it, does it not bleed? This wrist, this sweaty palm, this hand. How much? |
| ARCHER: | But we only have . . . |
| ARTUNIAN: | Sold! But I'm afraid you'll have to wrap it yourself. |
| DR F: | Gentlemen, thanks to Mr. Artunian's hand, we've been saved from Bat City, and we're off into the jungle in search of Shangra Deelite. |

**TRANSITION OF JUNGLE SOUNDS, ENDING WITH A ROAR**

| | |
|---|---|
| LEO: | What's that? |
| ARCHER: | It's a great horned carnivorous ibex. |
| HARRY: | Good heavens! |

**SOUND OF A BIRD**

| | |
|---|---|
| LEO: | What was that? |

**SWISH AND CRY**

| | |
|---|---|
| ARCHER: | It's a Giant Sumatran Gliding Rat. Poisonous! |

***Typical arrival ceremony in Bat City***

| | |
|---|---|
| **HARRY:** | It should be. |

**HORRIFIC NOISE**

| | |
|---|---|
| **LEO:** | What was that? |
| **DR F:** | That was Mr. Archer. He just fell into the rhino pit. |
| **HARRY:** | I've had enough of this Zoo. |
| **DR F:** | We're ready to face the jungle. Come on men. |

**SOUND OF BEATING DRUMS**

| | |
|---|---|
| **ARCHER:** | I remember my last crash with a rhino. It was in the Portland Zoo in ought '19. It was a much smaller beast, of course, with only one horn . . . |

| | |
|---|---|
| **DR F:** | Quiet, Mr. Archer! Don't you hear the drums? We must be in headhunter country. Who's got the map? |
| **HARRY:** | I have. It's in my pocket, trying to steal my loose change. |
| **DR F:** | Give it to me! Look! It's pointing back the way we came |
| **ARCHER:** | I think it's trying to tell us something. |
| **HARRY:** | It's quivering. Its palm is all sweaty. This hand is really nervous. It's trying to make me bite its nails! |
| **ARCHER:** | It's pointing to that tree on our right. |
| **HARRY:** | But that tree was just on our left. |
| **ARCHER:** | Listen. The drums have stopped. |
| **DR F:** | That's no tree, boys! It's an Indigenous Headhunter. |
| **LEO:** | How do you know? |
| **DR F:** | I can tell by the brass plate on the trunk — "Homo Indigenous, Donated by Mrs. Gerald Fitzpatrick, In Memory of an Endless Summer at Newport, 1924." |
| **ART:** | mrmrmrmrmrmr |
| **DR F:** | Don't worry, Art. We'll guard you with your life! Everyone inside the buffalo! Here they come! |
| **HEADHUNTER:** | Hiya, baby! What's happenin'? |
| **HARRY:** | I think they've spotted us! |
| **DR F:** | Right! We're all covered with spots. |
| **HEADHUNTER:** | Man, you really on the spot! |
| **HARRY:** | We actors. You headhunters. |
| **HEADHUNTER:** | Hmm. Ever since Inca go underground, we lonely, we look for heads. You give us hand, man? |

| | |
|---|---|
| **DR F:** | Yes, here's a man's hand. |
| **HEADHUNTER:** | Aggggg! What bummer! (FADES OFF) |
| **DR F:** | Thank god, they've gone! |
| **ART:** | mrmrmrmrmrm |
| **HARRY:** | Oh, they've upset poor Art! |
| **ARCHER:** | Well, we could entertain him with Act Two of The Count of Monte Cristo. I've been rehearsing it for the last seven pages. |
| **ART:** | mrmrmrmrmrmr |
| **DR F:** | Well, then, let's play him some music. What would you like to hear, Art? |
| **ART:** | mrmrmrmrmrmr |
| **LEO:** | What's his favorite group? The Buffalo Butter Conspiracy? |
| **ART:** | mrmrmrmrmr |
| **HARRY:** | No. What about the Jimmy Buffalo Experience? |
| **ART:** | mrmrmrmrmr |
| **ARCHER:** | Rhinoceros Springfield? |
| **ART:** | mrmrmrmrmr |
| **DR F:** | Capt. Beefheart and his Magic Buffalo? |
| **ART:** | mrmrmrmrmr |
| **HARRY:** | He's drooling. Quick, play it! |
| **MUSIC CUE:** | ABBA ZABBA |
| **DR F:** | Gimme three . . . |

**ARCHER:** I pass . . .

**HARRY:** I'll stick with what I've got . . .

**LEO:** Hit me!

**PAUSE . . . SOCK!**

**LEO:** Why, you cheatin' varmint! I saw you deal that Jack from the bottom of the deck. I want another hand!

**DR F:** Here, take this one.

**LEO:** Aggggggggggh!

**ARCHER:** What's this severed hand doing in the Last Chant Saloon?

**DR F:** What are we doing in the Last Chant Saloon?

**HARRY:** Hey, this is next week's show!

**DR F:** Where did we leave the plot for this week's show?

**ARCHER:** On page 15.

**DR F:** Well, it's too late to turn back now. Forward! Into the jungle! Forward!

**ALL:** Forward!

**DR F:** Wait a moment! Where are we going?

**ARCHER:** If someone will unclench this map from around my throat, I'll tell you . . . aggghhh!

**LEO:** What does it say?

**ARCHER:** The directions carefully hidden in this lavender birthmark can bring us no further in our search for Shangra Deelite.

**LEO:** Wait! The hand is trying to write something in the sand.

**HARRY:** Is it a love letter?

| | |
|---|---|
| **DR F:** | No, it's a message. |
| **ARCHER:** | What does it say? |
| **LEO:** | U C N G T M O P A . . . you can get mo pay . . . |
| **DR F:** | It's speed writing! |
| **ARCHER:** | Who gave this hand an upper? |
| **HARRY:** | Ha! We've got the upper hand! |
| **DR F:** | And we're hopelessly lost in this steaming jungle! |
| **LEO:** | Anybody got any clams? |
| **HARRY:** | What are we going to do, now that the hand has no more to say? |
| **ARCHER:** | Let's follow that freeway over there. |
| **DR F:** | Too obvious. |
| **ART:** | mrmrmrmrmr! |
| **HARRY:** | There goes the buffalo! |
| **DR F:** | Of course! Why didn't we think of it before? We'll follow that magnificent beast as he follows his own native instincts, reverting to the call of the wild, unhindered by the limitations of the over-conceptualized, convoluted, mechanistic modern mind of man! |
| **APPLAUSE** | |
| **DR F:** | After him! |
| **LEO:** | Dr. Firesign? |
| **DR F:** | What is it, Leo? |
| **LEO:** | He's gone. |

**GROANS**

**OLD MAN:** Help! Help! Over here! Help! Help!

**DR F:** Quick, gentlemen! Follow that hysterical cry for help help!

**ARCHER:** Press on through the underbrush!

**DR F:** I've never liked the underbrush press!

**SOUNDS OF CRASHING THROUGH UNDERBRUSH**

**LEO:** Oh! Look at that horrible hairy man!

**ARCHER:** Why, the poor man must be completely out of his mind from the heat, wearing a heavy coat in this weather!

**OLD MAN:** Help me! I've got a buffalo on my back! Won't someone help me, please! If I get out of this, I promise I'll never smoke another drop! Give me a hand!

**PAUSE . . . APPLAUSE**

**OLD MAN:** No! No! Give me a hand!

**DR F:** Here, take this one!

**OLD MAN:** Why, where did you get this? It's just like my map, only the thumb's on the other side. At last! I have it all! For 40 years, I've been wandering through this steaming jungle with no clams and Artunian's right hand, in search of the Lost City of Shangra Deelite. And now — I'll just put both hands together . . . Ah! I see it all now! You just make a left turn instead of a right when you get to AGGGRRH!

**ARCHER:** The poor devil. Strangled by his own map. It nearly happened to me . . .

**HARRY:** What did the old man say? Ah, I remember! Turn left instead of right at ARRRGGH!

**DR F:** And here we are!

**GASPS OF WONDER**

| | |
|---|---|
| **LAMA:** | (CHANTS) Don't die tonight. Call Shangra Deelite! |
| **ARCHER:** | Where did that voice come from? |
| **LAMA:** | Welcome gentle friends. Welcome to Shangra Deelite. |
| **ALL:** | Shangra Deelite!! |
| **LAMA:** | We deliver. Bring your shaggy four-legged friend, too. There's room for all in Shangra Deelite. |
| **HARRY:** | This is marvelous! Never have I seen a more beautiful place! |
| **ARCHER:** | It's like playing the last act of Camille, all rolled into one! |
| **LAMA:** | Playing? What's that? |
| **DR F:** | My dear man — we're actors. |
| **LAMA:** | Actors? What's that? |
| **LEO:** | You know — the bright lights. The grease paint, the glamour, the applause . . . |
| **HARRY:** | The curtain going up on the first act . . . |
| **ARCHER:** | You going up in the second act . . . |
| **DR F:** | The audience getting up in the third act . . . |
| **HARRY:** | The playwright giving up in the fourth act . . . |
| **ARCHER:** | The cast throwing up in the fifth act . . . |
| **DR F:** | And the sixth act . . . |
| **ALL:** | Bat City! |
| **LAMA:** | No offence, but I don't understand a word you're saying, and neither do any of my people assembled here before you. |
| **HARRY:** | Look! Finally, an audience worthy of us. |

*A typical ceremony for strangers arriving in Shangra Deelitl*

| | |
|---|---|
| **ARCHER:** | Larger than the Winter Palace in Spring. |
| **DR F:** | Gentlemen, do you think we could . . . |
| **LAMA:** | Of course you can. |
| **ARCHER:** | No, we can't. Where are we going to get The King? We always hire a local actor for that one line, but these people are too small to fit the costume. |
| **DR F:** | But the show must go on. |
| **LAMA:** | Show? |
| **ART:** | mrmrmrmrmrmr |

| | |
|---|---|
| **HARRY:** | Of course! We can use Art! He's a trooper. |
| **DR F:** | But can he learn the line? |
| **ARCHER:** | He's been practicing it for months! I've been holding book for him. He's ready. |
| **DR F:** | Good! Get him into the King Louis the 14th costume. We're about to play for our greatest audience. |
| **LAMA:** | Audience? |
| **DR F:** | Go tell all of your people assembled here before us that they've just got to be some of the most beautiful people in the whole wide world! |
| **LAMA:** | It's true. It's true. It's true. |
| **ARCHER:** | And we love you. And you'll love us, if you'll just turn around and watch the show. |

**GENERAL HUBUB**

| | |
|---|---|
| **DR F:** | Good evening. May I present for your edification and enjoyment, an evening with Dr. Firesign's Original Traveling Antique Theatre of the Plains and Buffalo Show, in their immortal classic, "Waiting For The Count of Monte Cristo, or Someone Like Him." The Scene — another part of the street, outside the alley, under the cul-de-sac, adjoining the antechamber, near the courtyard, in the palace, by the moonlight, wa da doo dah. Guelph speaks . . . |
| **HARRY:** | (WAKING) What place is this? |
| **ARCHER:** | Never mind. You are in safe hands. |
| **HARRY:** | Get your hands off me, old man. Do you know who I am? |
| **ARCHER:** | Far better than you, Edmond Dantes. Know now the secret of your birth — you are the only legitimate son of . . . |

**DAGGER TOSSED INTO BACK**

ARCHER: . . . of . . . aggggggagagagagghhh! (DIES)

HARRY: I don't know any aaaaghgghggghh! My father's name was arararrrghgh. (AFTER A SILENCE) Dr. Firesign — they hate us out there!

DR F: Quick! Cut to the dueling scene.

LEO: Dantes Ha! Here you are! And here I am! Take that, you swine!

HARRY: Why, this is not my swine!

LEO: Then, on guard, you blaggard!

## DUEL IN WHICH LEO DIES

DR F: We're dying! Cut to the poison scene, they always love it.

HARRY: Bon jour M. Hemloque. (Now to fix this traitorous dog of my Uncle with some of his own medicine!) Sur la table!

DR F: Nephew!

HARRY: Gasundtheit!

DR F: Merci! Now, let us talk of your late father's estate.

HARRY: Isn't it a little late for that? Let's share a flagon of churning burgundy first. You first.

## HE POISONS THE CUP, THE UNCLE DRAINS THE GLASS, IS STABBED

DR F: Just like his brother. A heavy hand with the cyanide. Now, I shall run him through with my dagger.

## DISCOVERS HIS DAGGER, DIES

HARRY: Oh! They hate us. They really hate us. But the confrontation with the King never fails to bring tears to their eyes.

ARCHER: His Majesty, the King!

ART: mrmrmrmrmrmr

| | |
|---|---|
| **HARRY:** | Father! |
| **ART:** | mrmrmrmrmrmr |

**BURST OF APPLAUSE AND BRAVOS**

| | |
|---|---|
| **VOICES:** | The buffalo! We want the buffalo! |
| **LAMA:** | Now we know what acting is. You're terrible! But the buffalo is brilliant! We've decided to let you off with your lives, if you'll leave the buffalo here. |
| **DR F:** | At last! We've found a place where Art is appreciated. Well, gentlemen, we might as well push on. There's nothing left but Bat City. |
| **LAMA:** | What did you say? |
| **DR F:** | Bat City. |
| **LAMA:** | But you've just played Bat City. Shangra Deelite means, in our language, "gathering place of the sub-audible flying mouse." |
| **DR F:** | Well, Mr. Archer? |
| **ARCHER:** | Yes, Dr. Firesign? |
| **DR F:** | After all these years, we've finally played Bat City. |
| **ARCHER:** | From now on it's all up hill. |
| **BOY:** | Hey! Dr. Firestein! I got another telegram for you or your buffalo. |
| **DR F:** | I'll take it, boy. |
| **BOY:** | You sure will! Stand back, it's another singing one. It's from all the people of Shangra Deelite. |
| **VOICES (SINGING):** | B A T – C I T – Y - Spells bye to you. So long! Good bye! |

**ANNOUNCER:** The Firesign Theatre has presented NONE OF THE ABOVE. Do you believe in buffalos? Say quick that you believe. If you believe, clap your hands!

**BOWS**

*for Orson*

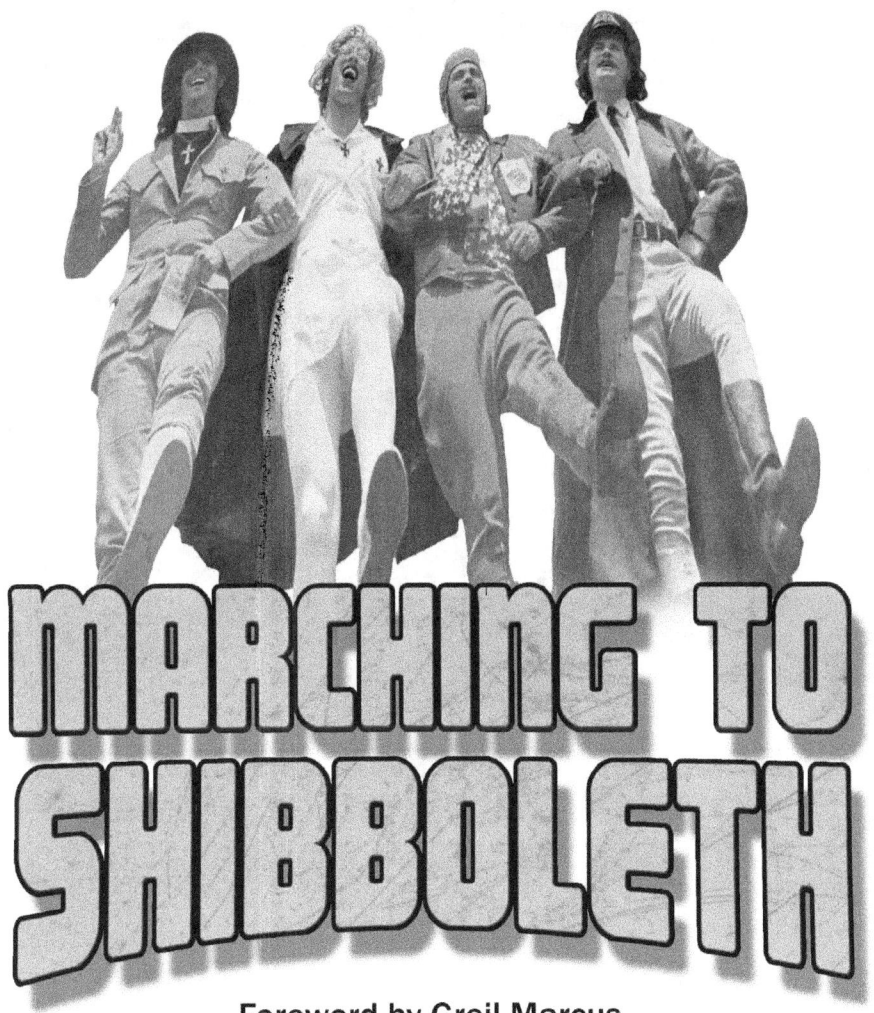

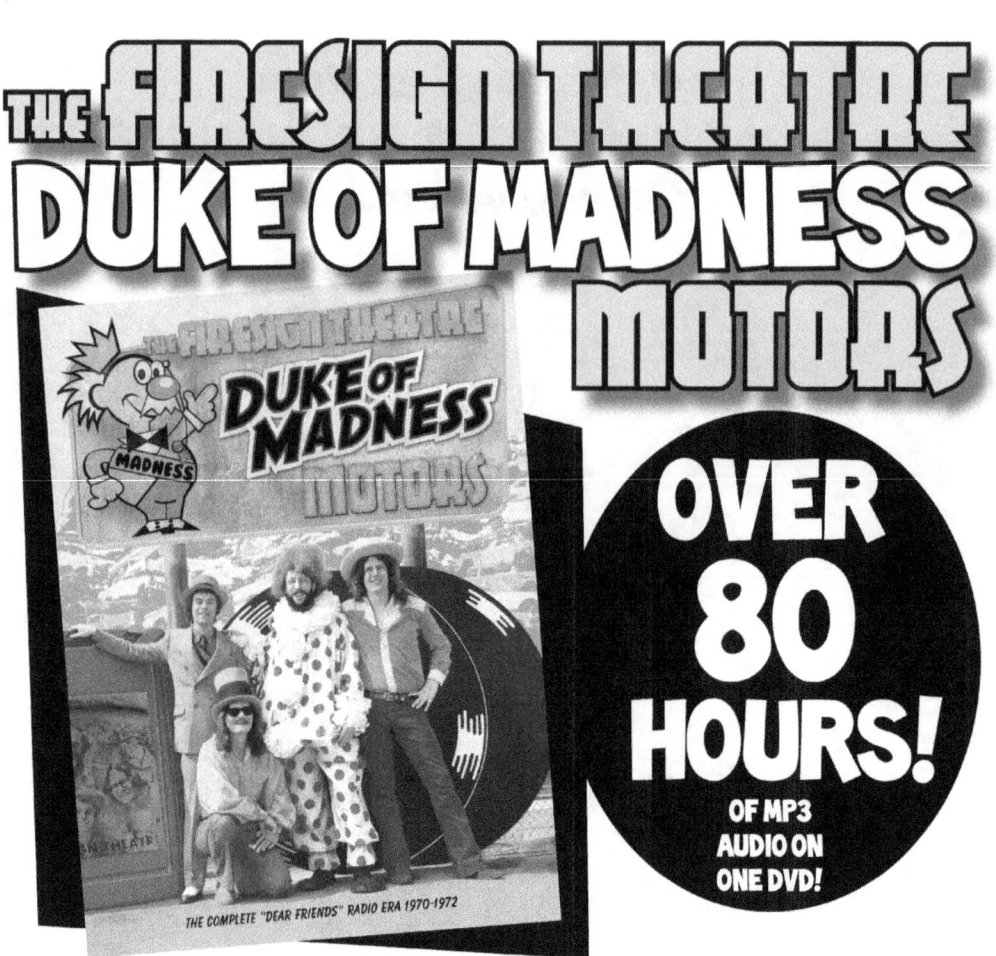

# FROM 1/4 OF THE MINDS OF FIRESIGN THEATRE...

## THE RONALD REAGAN MURDER CASE
### A GEORGE TIREBITER MYSTERY

"A lively and entertaining read"
- *Norman Corwin*
"It looks to be a hell of a lot of fun"
- *Ray Bradbury*

## DR. FIRESIGN'S FOLLIES

The Art of Radio
Surrealist Comedy
Tirebiter's Mystery
Firesign History

Order your copies today!
**bearmanormedia.com • firesigntheatre.com**

www.ingramcontent.com/pod-product-compliance
Lightning Source LLC
Chambersburg PA
CBHW081146230426
43664CB00018B/2827